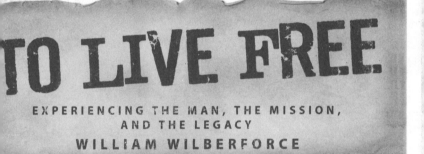

TO LIVE FREE

EXPERIENCING THE MAN, THE MISSION, AND THE LEGACY

WILLIAM WILBERFORCE

TO LIVE FREE

EXPERIENCING THE MAN, THE MISSION, AND THE LEGACY
WILLIAM WILBERFORCE

BARBOUR
PUBLISHING

Published by Barbour Publishing, Inc., P.O. Box 719, Uhrichsville, Ohio 44683, www.barbourbooks.com

Our mission is to publish and distribute inspirational products offering exceptional value and biblical encouragement to the masses.

ecpa Member of the
Evangelical Christian
Publishers Association

Printed in the United States of America.
5 4 3 2 1

To former U.S. Senator Mark Hatfield,
who in so many ways reflected Wilberforce's
political courage and commitment to Christ.

CONTENTS

INTRODUCTION

Perhaps you're already familiar with the life and work of William Wilberforce. Or maybe this book will be a first introduction to the man, his mission, and his legacy. Whatever your starting point, you will no doubt come away with an appreciation for this eighteenth- and nineteenth-century English politician, one of a group of people we call the Illuminators—faithful believers who carried the light of Jesus Christ to their world.

Wilberforce is best known for his effort to abolish slavery in the British Empire. But he was also a deeply committed Christian who tried to apply biblical principles to all of society. In this book, you'll read a novelized biography that touches on these major themes of his life. The story casts light on the beliefs and values that made William Wilberforce a force for good, challenging us in the twenty-first century to "go and do likewise" (Luke 10:37 NIV).

To Live Free also provides thought-provoking insights from Wilberforce's spiritual writing—topical excerpts from a book he originally titled *The Practical View of the Prevailing Religious Systems of Professed Christians in the Higher and Middle Classes of This Country Contrasted with Real Christianity.* These excerpts, inserted into relevant locations in the biography, are taken from an updated and abridged edition of Wilberforce's book simply titled *Real Christianity.*

It is our hope that you'll be inspired by William Wilberforce's example, challenged to live a life that pleases God and benefits humanity.

THE EDITORS

1

VICTORY

July 26, 1833

The late afternoon shadows that threatened to overwhelm the tidy sitting room were suddenly pierced by a ray of light from an open doorway. Sensing the change, the elderly man who was all but swallowed up by his wing chair turned his head.

"Zachary, is that you?"

In three strides, the visitor entered the room and clasped his hand on the frail man's shoulder. "Good news, William! God has truly answered your prayers."

"Yes, I heard about the vote in Parliament. I've been thanking God since the word came." Still,

William Wilberforce looked less than pleased.

That day, even though Parliament had over-whelmingly voted to eliminate the slave trade and support abolition, the old man knew better than almost anyone that true abolition would be many years away. Slavery was still ongoing in the British colonies. Moreover, Wilberforce was especially loath to heap any credit for the victory on himself. Countless people had labored for years to reach this goal, including his distinguished visitor and longtime friend, Zachary Macaulay. But the victory—when it truly came for the beleaguered slaves—would be God's.

Macaulay gave his friend a concerned look. Certain that Wilberforce did not have long to live, he knew the victory must be sweet for Wilberforce despite his humility. Wilberforce's body had been weakened by numerous ailments, but it was apparent that he still possessed a keen mind and was fully aware of what was happening in the world. He had so much to teach! Macaulay settled back in his chair and waved his hand, as if encouraging him to expound. "Tell me what you're thinking, William. Heaven knows, there are many distinguished—and not so distinguished—members of Parliament who would love to hear your stories, especially after this auspicious day."

Wilberforce narrowed his eyes as if trying to discern Macaulay's true motives. "What's wrong, Zachary? Don't you think I'm going to live much longer? Well, if it's stories you want. . .though it's likely you've heard them all before. Will you promise to stop me if I tell you more than you want to know?"

As if summoned by a bell, one of William's grandsons then brought tea and biscuits for the two men. As surreptitiously as possible, he also checked to make sure the slight man was comfortable. Satisfied for the moment, he then departed silently.

WILLIAM WILBERFORCE ON EMOTIONS

We can barely look anywhere in the Bible without finding abundant proof that God wants us to experience a faith that includes our emotions. Love, zeal, gratitude, joy, hope, trust (each one of them mentioned in the Bible) were not given to us to make us weak; instead, we are even commanded to experience these emotions as part of our faith's duties. They are an integral part of the worship that is acceptable to God.

William Wilberforce closed his eyes as if trying to collect his thoughts. He must not waste an opportunity to share the real motivation behind his quest for the abolition of slavery—that the only way he had kept going all these years was because of the hand of God nudging him forward.

Wilberforce had been well into his political career before he saw any need to surrender his life to Christ as Savior and Lord. He had been elected to a seat in Parliament from Hull, a North Sea port, when he was twenty-one years old, just old enough to serve. Then the opportunity came to move up and win one of the county seats from Yorkshire, which was about twenty times as large as Hull. On March 25, 1784, the Yorkshire Association called a meeting of the voters of the district to solicit support for reforms in Parliament and get more backing for Prime Minister William Pitt. Wilberforce went to York to help the cause of his friend Pitt, whom he had known from Cambridge and had been working with in the House of Commons. No one at the York meeting, including Wilberforce, expected that the day would end with his being positioned as a likely choice for one of the two Yorkshire seats.

"Four thousand voters showed up that day, Zachary, even though it was miserably cold," Wilberforce mused. "And not only did they show up, but they stayed through the whole day to hear all of the speakers!" He went on to explain that the organizers of the meeting wanted the group to adopt a petition to the king, asking for an immediate election. This tactic was meant to give prominence to the reform goals of the Yorkshire Association and help William Pitt's supporters win seats in the House of Commons.

The speeches continued on through the afternoon, with all the important people in Yorkshire being given a chance to speak. Wilberforce's district of Hull was within Yorkshire, even though it was separate for the purpose of representation in the Commons, so some of his constituents were there that day. Still, no one thought he would be given an opportunity to speak. At about four o'clock in the afternoon, his turn finally came. It was actually not much of an honor to be given the platform when the crowd was tired, cold, and restless. Wilberforce half expected that most of the people would leave before he could get much said. To his surprise, the people became quiet and listened to him. He was able to hold their attention for nearly an hour.

"When I was about to bring my speech to a close,

I saw a commotion on the edge of the crowd," he said. He thought at first it was a group starting to head home, but he soon realized that a messenger from the king was trying to reach the platform. "I motioned him forward and took it on myself to read the message, and it could not have been better news. The king had dissolved Parliament the day before, and the election was going to happen in the near future!" Wilberforce called on the group to join forces behind the efforts for reform and to assure that Prime Minister Pitt would be able to continue giving his strong leadership. Not only was there great support in the crowd for this proposition, but some in the crowd began to shout out that Wilberforce should be considered for one of Yorkshire's two seats. Prior to that, he was a literal unknown in most of Yorkshire, but within days a canvass was held, and he got one of the seats.

"God works in amazing ways, even for those who don't acknowledge Him. Don't you ever forget that, Macaulay," Wilberforce admonished his friend.

Macaulay leaned forward. "I take it your conversion experience was as dramatic as your selection to the Yorkshire seat in Commons?" He had heard the story many times, but it was obvious his friend relished retelling the tale. He would not deny him that pleasure, not on this auspicious day.

"No, it was not dramatic at all," Wilberforce replied. "If you're hoping to hear about something like the apostle Paul's conversion on the road to Damascus, you are going to be disappointed." Wilberforce smiled. "Actually, my spiritual rebirth did happen on a road, but there was no blinding light or voice from God. It was on the road to and from the coast of France that God began to speak to me."

Wilberforce began to describe the process of accompanying his mother, sister, and two cousins on their way to France. The trip required a long carriage ride to the port, a passage by ship across the English Channel, and then another carriage ride to Nice. Even though Wilberforce had plenty to attend to in his new duties representing Yorkshire, it would have been unthinkable to send the women of his family off without a male escort to look after their needs.

"You see, I needed to find a companion for myself, someone I could talk to on the way, someone who would help with the arrangements," he said, clearing his throat slightly. "I was getting a little desperate, to be honest, so I asked someone I didn't know very well—Isaac Milner, a lecturer at Cambridge, who had been a teacher at the primary school I attended. Extremely bright chap. I was confident that the trip would be interesting at the very least."

What Wilberforce didn't know was that Milner had become what the young Parliament member and his friends scoffingly called a Methodist. Wilberforce and his friends felt that these Methodists, or evangelicals, were way off track. They talked about the need for a conversion experience quite apart from one's baptism into the church as a child. That seemed ridiculous to Wilberforce. Besides, the evangelicals seemed to put way too much emphasis on emotionalism. Religion to Wilberforce was a part of one's social obligations. He had no great problem with the sermons he heard in church, but the talk about Jesus forgiving one's sins seemed totally absurd.

"So did Isaac Milner try to convert you to his type of evangelical faith?" Macaulay asked, playing along.

"Not really. He didn't even bring up the subject."

Wilberforce went on to explain that his favorite theologian at the time was one Theophilus Lindsey, who was the first in the Church of England to talk about God as one being, and not as part of the

Trinity. Unitarianism sounded great to a young intellectual who didn't want to deal with the many supernatural things in the New Testament.

On the journey to France, Wilberforce picked up a copy of a book by Philip Doddridge. He asked Milner what he thought of the book, and Milner said it was one of the best he had ever read. Milner and Wilberforce read it together and talked about it on the way home to England, and Wilberforce began to realize the truth of the gospel. But he still was not ready to make a commitment.

Isaac Milner agreed to accompany Wilberforce back to France to bring the women home at the end of the season. On the way they discussed the Bible and what it means to be a follower of Christ. They read and discussed the New Testament in Greek, because both of them had studied the language at Cambridge.

Wilberforce's repentance occurred over a period of months. Gradually he began to turn his back on his frivolous ways and began to meditate, pray, and write his thoughts and questions in a journal. By the end of the year, he had become a serious follower of Christ.

Macaulay looked at his friend with a question

WILLIAM WILBERFORCE ON SYMPATHY

All humanity suffers from the same desperate illness—and the Son of God has rescued us all. This knowledge should help us to feel sympathy toward all our fellow creatures. Immersed in the world's thinking, we too often notice the ways we are different; we identify more with the people who are like us in education and fortune, while we feel less sympathy for those who do not seem as similar to ourselves. But once we see that in the most important way we are all alike, we will begin to feel compassion for an unthinking world. Our prejudice and hatred soften and melt away; we are ashamed of thinking so much about the petty injuries which we may have suffered, when we consider what the Son of God—He "who did no sin, neither was guile found in his mouth" (1 Peter 2:22)—underwent so patiently.

written on his face. He didn't want to waste this opportunity, but he could see that it had been tiring for Wilberforce to tell the story.

"Something has bothered me all of these years. Why didn't you just go ahead and work for the abolition of slavery back in 1807, instead of settling for a bill that only outlawed British participation in the slave trade?"

Wilberforce nodded his head, as if expecting the question. Almost all of those involved in the abolition movement would have preferred to take care of the slavery problem all at once. They had worked in the cause for more than twenty years and had no desire to drag it out for another twenty-five, but in politics one has to settle for modest steps toward accomplishing a larger goal. As strong as the support for slavery was, they never would have succeeded in passing emancipation in 1807. They had to settle for putting an end to the trade while trusting that the public conscience would begin to understand that slavery itself was the evil, not just slave trafficking.

On the night the 1807 abolition bill passed, Wilberforce hardly needed to say anything in Parliament. Most of the abolition efforts had been in the House of Commons, but in this case some very clever planning in the House of Lords resulted in the successful attaching of an abolition measure to another bill that was expected to get the support of the proslavery forces. It worked, removing the possibility of the House of Lords blocking action at a later time.

When the discussion proceeded in Commons, it seemed almost anticlimactic; government ministers backed the abolition measure. So dramatic was the shift toward support of the measure, only sixteen members voted against it. Wilberforce couldn't believe his ears when the vote was announced. He went home early that morning with inexpressible joy that he had been able to see the first major victory in the greatest of his life callings. He gave all the glory to God that night. "Praise His name for putting it into the hearts of our politicians to finally do the right thing," Wilberforce said.

"And now you have your victory at last," summed up Macaulay before taking his leave. "I'm sorry to have tired you, but what you have told me is most enlightening—and I think, just the beginning of an even better story."

After saying good night to his friend, Wilberforce gazed out through the lace curtains at the tidy garden at his cousin's house. He was only staying here to be near his doctors, but the setting was perfectly compatible with his thoughts. Indeed, he was used to being uprooted. . .and he remembered the first time like it was yesterday.

This is what the LORD says—your Redeemer, the Holy One of Israel: "I am the LORD your God, who teaches you what is best for you, who directs you in the way you should go."

ISAIAH 48:17 NIV

2

THE ROAD TO CAMBRIDGE

He felt almost suffocated by the embrace, his face pushed against the coarse fabric of his uncle's waistcoat. Then it was his aunt's turn to throw her arms around him. Her muslin housedress smelled like a loaf of fresh bread.

"Willy, Uncle William and I will do our best to make you feel at home," Aunt Hannah whispered. The names in the Wilberforce family were confusing. Both young William's uncle and his grandfather were also named William. And the younger William later named his oldest son William.

Nine-year-old William Wilberforce wanted desperately to believe her. To him, tragedy seemed everywhere recently. Just the year before, in 1767, his sister Elizabeth had died at the age of fourteen. Elizabeth had been away at a boarding school for most of Willy's growing-up years, but he had treasured the times she was home.

Soon after the death of his sister, Willy lost his father, Robert Wilberforce, who was only forty when he died. Robert had been in the family businesses of banking and trade with Europe. Willy hadn't felt close to his father, but the loss of two of his immediate family members in a few months had been difficult. Dealing with the death of his loved ones made William even more conscious of his own physical limitations. He was

WORLD EVENTS OF 1768

English explorer James Cook begins his first voyage across the Pacific Ocean.

Citizens of Boston refuse to house British soldiers.

Dolley Madison, wife of the fourth U.S. president, is born in the colony of North Carolina.

Italian artist Canaletto dies.

slight of build, not at all strong, and had poor eyesight.

William and Hannah felt more than pity for the young boy who came to join their household in London. God had not blessed them with children of their own, so they were delighted to have Willy to love and care for. They saw a boy with a strong mind that made up for his weak body. They were impressed with his wit and his ability to express himself far better than one would expect from a boy of nine. They hoped they could provide some important spiritual nurture for him, too.

After tea was served and Willy's things delivered to his new room at the spacious Wilberforce house on St. James Place, Willy's uncle discussed the plans he and Hannah had made for him. Already they had spoken to Mr. Chambers, headmaster at Putney School, and were assured there was a place for Willy at the school. Willy had done well at Hull Grammar School, particularly because of the teaching of young Joseph Milner. They assured their nephew that the teachers at Putney would be able to challenge his mind and that he would make many friends there. He would have classes in writing, French, arithmetic, Latin, and a little Greek. "You have a great future in the Wilberforce family businesses, young man," Uncle William promised.

Willy tried to focus on what his uncle was saying, but he had other things on his mind. "Uncle William, I remember coming to visit you at your place in Wimbledon. I loved being in your garden with all the birds singing. Can we go there soon?"

Uncle William couldn't help but laugh. "Soon, my boy, very soon. First, though, we've got to get you settled at school. God willing, during the holidays we'll go to Wimbledon. Having you here—" William cleared his throat to cover his transparent emotions— "I mean, God has blessed us very much, and we want to do everything to make you happy."

WILLIAM WILBERFORCE ON HUMAN WEAKNESS

Those who have formed a true picture of their lost and helpless condition will be glad to listen to the sound of His voice, and they will accurately judge the infinite value of their deliverance. And that is why it is so important that we not skim over humanity's weakness and corruption, even though it is painful and humiliating to realize just how needy we all are. Looking at this reality is hard for us, and we tend to be filled with a mixture of anger and disgust—but given our condition, this pain is good for us. Like the hard lessons that adversity teaches us, the consequences are permanently helpful to our souls.

Almost two weeks had passed since Willy arrived in London, and he knew he had to write to his mother, Elizabeth.

Dearest Mum,

Uncle and Auntie have been very kind to me, and I'm doing well. They send you their love. I like my room at their house on St. James Place, and they have promised we will go to Wimbledon during the first holiday. Maybe you can join us there. I wish I could say I liked my school, but that would not be true. The classes are not nearly as interesting as those at Hull, and the food makes me ill. There is this despicable man on the school staff who is supposed to keep us in order. He's Scottish, and he seems intent on showing us that we English are somehow inferior to the Scots. But I suppose I'll be okay, Mum. I miss you. Give my love to Sarah and give an extra hug to Ann. Aunt Hannah is going to come for me next weekend. She said we would go to visit her brother, John Thornton, at Clapham. There is a church there she says I will enjoy. Bye for now.

Your loving son, Willy

One year later, Willy's letter reflected his growing interest in religion.

> *Dearest Mum,*
>
> *My visit to Hull was grand. Mum, you remember when I first arrived I told you about going with Aunt Hannah to her brother's church in Clapham? We've gone there several times since. Some of the people there call themselves "Methodists," but I'm not quite sure what that means. I suspect you might not like some of the things they are teaching in their church.*
>
> *We went to church at Clapham again last Sunday, and the guest minister was very interesting. His name is John Newton. He's the rector at Olney in Buckinghamshire. For a parson, he has had a most amazing life. He talked about his days at sea and how God had delivered him from terrible circumstances. He became captain of a slave ship, but now he has asked God to forgive him for being so cruel to the people of Africa. He said he had come to understand that slavery was sinful and had asked God to forgive him for his past and to help him treat people more lovingly. He made me want*

to commit my life to Jesus. I hope you can come
to hear him preach sometime.

Until later, your loving son, Willy

Willy's seemingly innocent letter was read and reread by his mother, who then promptly summoned her father-in-law. On a cold, drizzly day in Hull, Elizabeth poured tea for the elderly man as he slowly scanned his grandson's missive.

"Willy seems to have taken up with the Enthusiasts in Clapham that William and Hannah admire so much," Elizabeth said. "I don't think I dare leave him there any longer."

Elizabeth was a loyal member of the Church of England, at least on a social level. She and others of wealth disdained both the theology and the social class of the followers of John Wesley. Two decades before Willy's birth, John Wesley, himself a loyal member of the Church of England, had a profound spiritual experience. He spoke of his heart being "strangely warmed" and of trusting in Christ for salvation. He believed that his sins had been forgiven by faith alone, not by his baptism as a child. At the time Willy was attending services in Clapham, the name Methodist was used interchangeably with the term "Enthusiast"—a person who was far too emotional about his or her spirituality and put too much emphasis on salvation and forgiveness of sins. An even greater problem for Elizabeth Wilberforce was the fact that most Methodists were from the lower classes.

William and Hannah were close friends of George Whitefield, who was making quite an impression on people of wealth. Elizabeth didn't think Willy had heard Whitefield preach, but John Newton was a Methodist, and his talk of forgiveness from sins, personal salvation, and faith alone went against all she had learned in the church about the sacraments and the baptism of children as the way to confirm one's faith.

When Willy's grandfather had finished reading, he raised his head and peered at Elizabeth, who was trying hard to gauge his reaction. "You're right, Elizabeth," he said, nodding his head. "Your son carries my name, and he won't get a penny of my inheritance if he continues down this Methodist pathway. William and Hannah won't like it if you take him from their care, but you really must. There's so much at stake for the future of our family. How disgusting it would be for Willy to become a Methodist!"

WILLIAM WILBERFORCE ON CHRISTIAN UNITY

Cultivate a spirit of goodwill for everyone. Join in friendly fellowship with all people of faith, whatever their sect or denomination. If you find you differ from them in some areas, remember that so long as you agree on faith's central doctrine, the rest is nonessential. Respect people of real spirituality wherever they are found, and encourage others to grow in their faith. Do all you can to help revive and spread the influence of faith and virtue. Pray earnestly and constantly that your efforts will be successful.

On the quiet coach ride home to Hull, Willy's emotions were heavy. As he thought about the terrible scene when his mother informed his aunt and uncle that she was taking Willy home, he tried not to show his sadness and anger. He desperately wished he hadn't written to his mother about John Newton's sermons at Clapham—and worse, his own attraction to the Methodists' message. He should have known how his mother and grandfather would react. Loudly and often they had bemoaned the spiritual excesses of the lower classes.

Willy was so upset, words sputtered out. "B–b–but you saw how upset Uncle William and Aunt Hannah were by my having to leave. They have no children of their own. And I've gotten used to the school at Putney. If I promise not to go back to the church at Clapham, could I return to live with Uncle and Auntie?"

"Of course not, William. You have no idea what it would do to your future as a member of the Wilberforce family if you continued with this Methodist nonsense. Your father would have been shocked by what you've done and said. I owe it to him to rescue you from these terrible influences."

"Can I go back to Hull School? I really liked that school." At the look his mother gave him, he immediately regretted asking one more question. The answer was immediate.

"The new headmaster, Joseph Milner, has become

a Methodist. It's already been arranged. You will go to your grandfather's old school at Pocklington. Be assured that Reverend Kingsman Baskett, the headmaster, will not tolerate any Methodism."

Nothing about the forced relocation to Pocklington School was to the liking of twelve-year-old William Wilberforce. He missed the affection and spiritual nurture of his aunt and uncle. He wrote words of encouragement to his uncle that reflected his own loneliness and spiritual discouragement: "Comfort yourself, you Dearest, that they who are in Jesus must suffer Persecution and it is just as it should be; if we suffer with him we shall also reign with him; and let what will happen he is blessed who has the Lord for his hope, who can look unto him as unto a loving father being reconciled to him by the blood of Jesus."[1]

Young William later said of the school at Pocklington, "The Master was a good sort of man and rather an elegant scholar but the boys were a sad set. . . . I did nothing at all there."[2]

The void in Wilberforce's intellectual and spiritual life during his five years at Pocklington School was gradually filled with his increased access to the wealth of his family and the abundant social opportunities in

Hull. While it did not measure up to London, some called Hull the "Dublin of England" because of its many theaters, balls, lavish dinners, and card parties. During school holidays, Willy's life consisted of a daily routine of dinner at two, tea at six, card playing until nine, then a lavish supper. Willy's grandfather died during this time, and since Willy had by all appearances left his Methodism behind, his grandfather left him a more-than-comfortable inheritance. The abundance of money and leisure time made Willy a favored social companion, as did his conversational skills and his remarkable singing voice.

The fading of Wilberforce's earlier spiritual interests was of his own doing, but he had plenty of help. He later said of this process:

> As grandson of one of the principal inhabitants,
> I was everywhere invited and caressed: My voice
> and love of music made me still more acceptable.
> The religious impressions that I gained at Wimbledon continued for a considerable time, but my
> friends spared no pains to stifle them. I might
> almost say that no pious parent ever laboured
> more to impress a beloved child with sentiments

of piety than they did to give me a taste of the world and its diversions.[3]

Wilberforce's preference for social activities over academic and spiritual development continued after he was admitted to St. John's College, Cambridge University. Given the social standing of his family and his completion of studies at a well-known school, it was not hard for Wilberforce to get into Cambridge. Once there, he discovered that a person of means could get along well at the university without letting studies interfere with his social life. Only those headed into careers in the law and the clergy were pushed toward intellectual rigor. He said of his initiation into life at Cambridge:

> *I was introduced, on the very first night of my arrival, to as licentious a set of men as can well be conceived. They drank hard, and their conversation was even worse than their lives. . . . But those with whom I was intimate did not act towards me the part of Christians, or even of honest men. Their object seemed to be to make and keep me idle.*[4]

WILLIAM WILBERFORCE ON INTELLECT

To the real Christian, the gospel's unique truths are the center to which she gravitates—the very sun of her solar system, the soul of the world. They are the origin of all that is excellent and lovely, the source of light and life, motion and warmth. From them come all creative energy. Our intellects would be cold and comfortless without their light and guidance.

Certainly Wilberforce made his own decisions about the use of his time and energies at Cambridge—and later came to regret the decisions he made. He was especially upset that his tutors did nothing to discourage his idleness at the university. They apparently assumed he would finish at Cambridge and slip into adulthood with all his material needs met and without much need for intellectual depth.

As on many evenings, Wilberforce returned to his room at St. John's, tired from a day of card playing, drinking, eating, singing, and conversation. The word at the time for witty repartee was "foining," and William got high marks at Cambridge as a foinster.

It was late, but he didn't want to go to bed yet, so he banged on the stove chimney in his room, summoning the student next door, Thomas Gisborne.

"You're studying far too hard, Gisborne," a laughing Wilberforce said. "You're going to completely wear out that brain of yours." Offering his neighbor a chair, Wilberforce tried to tempt the studious Gisborne with Yorkshire pie and ale. "You've already established yourself as one of our top students," Wilberforce said. "Why study so hard?"

"The examiners for the priesthood can be very tough," Gisborne replied, adding wistfully that he had not been blessed with the kind of money and business opportunities Wilberforce had. The ministry would offer Gisborne a secure position in the future, the chance to do good for humanity, and the opportunity to honor God.

Still, the serious Gisborne recognized the appeal of Wilberforce's life of pleasure. "You have it made," he told Wilberforce. "You're one of the most popular students in our college. You're a gifted speaker. You can sing. People love being around you."

"Well, I don't know about that," Wilberforce said, "but I envy your determination and your hard work. You know what? I have no real idea of where I'm headed in life."

The family businesses, with their comfortable incomes, awaited William Wilberforce if he chose to pursue them. But his heart wasn't in trade and banking. The world of politics was a possibility, all the more so since Wilberforce had met the energetic young William Pitt—a man starting a career that would one day lead to the prime minister's office. But Wilberforce had to admit that his own interest in politics lacked the clear direction that Pitt so obviously possessed.

"Well, I suspect you will find your purpose in life one of these days," Gisborne said with no real conviction. "Meanwhile, enjoy life, right?"

"I suppose so," William said, though even he couldn't summon enough sincerity to fool a classmate.

The truth was, he felt seduced into a life of idleness, partially by his tutors and friends, who seemed determined to keep him from applying himself. He told Gisborne about his years with his aunt and uncle. "I had every intention of committing my life to Christ as Savior and Lord. I think I actually did so, as much as a young boy could. But that life of spiritual zeal seems very distant from me now. Well, good night, Thomas. I'll not be blamed for keeping you from your studies as others have done to me. You will be going to lectures tomorrow. As you know, that's not my habit."

Later that night, William got up from his bed and began pacing the room. What direction would his life take? And why did he keep coming back to those years with his aunt and uncle?

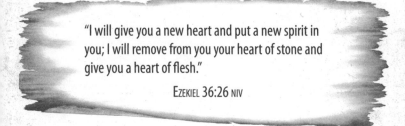

"I will give you a new heart and put a new spirit in you; I will remove from you your heart of stone and give you a heart of flesh."

EZEKIEL 36:26 NIV

3

POLITICS

As William searched for a seat in the gallery at the House of Commons, he spied a familiar face. "Excuse me, Mr. Pitt, do you mind if I join you? I don't know if you remember, but we met at Cambridge." William waited a few seconds, then plunged ahead. "I've seen you a number of times here in the gallery, and I suspect we may be here for the same reasons. Unless I'm mistaken, your goal is to be down there on the floor before long."

At last Pitt nodded. "I'm studying for the bar now—before I take my place, as you say, 'on the floor.' You're from Hull, aren't you? Is that where you would stand for election?"

"Yes, but nobody there thinks of me as a political

contender. What seat would you seek?"

"That's a problem. There's no logical place for me to run. I suppose I'll try in Cambridge, but my youth will be a problem there. Are you twenty-one yet?"

"Not until next August. If I were a praying man, I would pray that the elections wait until after my birthday."

"Timing is everything in politics, isn't it?" Pitt noted. "Well, it seems the members have exhausted their store of wisdom for the evening and are about to adjourn. Join me for a bite to eat?"

Wilberforce's entrance into politics was almost a random choice. The funds he inherited from his grandfather and uncle assured that he could be comfortable without additional income. Although he was the only son in his family and could have taken his father's place in the trading business, he had no interest in that career. There were cousins in the business who were more than happy to continue managing it.

The truth was, William had not applied himself adequately at the university to study for the bar, and he had no interest in being a clergyman. Medicine was out of the question because of his grades. The remaining option for a person of his class was a career in politics.

Wilberforce could not have come up with even a short list of issues that drew him into politics. People told him he was a good speaker. He was personable and popular, but he had a fairly limited understanding of the issues being debated in Parliament. He assumed he could become better informed with time, and toward that end he had been spending his time listening to the debates in Westminster Palace.

As Pitt said, in politics timing is everything. Although he wouldn't have given credit to God at the time, Wilberforce couldn't have been better served by the announcement that Parliament was dissolved and there would be new elections. Prime Minister Lord North actually made the dissolution announcement on Wilberforce's twenty-first birthday, assuring that he would be old enough to seek a seat in Parliament. Although he had no advance warning of the announcement, Wilberforce had already invited the people of Hull to help him celebrate his birthday at an ox roast.

It was common practice at the time to give cash payments to voters in exchange for their support. English political leaders viewed the practice as an expression of appreciation for those who intended to vote for them. The going rate was two guineas for a vote. Hull voters who lived in London and voted in Hull expected to receive ten guineas for the effort of coming home to cast their votes. The total cost for these payments and other campaign expenses was eight thousand pounds, a substantial sum for the average person, but Wilberforce had plenty of money to work with.

After the election, among the first to congratulate Wilberforce was William Pitt. "Wilberforce, my friend, what an impressive victory at Hull!" Pitt exclaimed. "I heard you got as many votes as the two incumbents combined."

"I'm sorry to hear that things didn't go as well for you in Cambridge. Are you in the process of arranging for a seat from one of the small boroughs?"

"Yes, but you might as well call it what everyone does—a rotten borough. The person whose borough I will represent has assured me I can operate independently in the House. I hope things will work out in time for me to take my seat in January."

"I have no doubt, Pitt, that your career will be far more impressive than mine."

WILLIAM WILBERFORCE ON LIFEWORK

No one, however, has the right to do nothing. We all have a great eternal work that we are called to accomplish; eternity demands that we use this short and precarious life as well as we can. But aside from that, in a world as needy as ours, surely health and leisure and financial wealth should be able to find some ignorance to instruct, some wrong to redress, some want to supply, some misery to alleviate. Won't ambition and greed ever go to sleep in our hearts? Will we never run out of things to want? We are so quick to discover new things to desire, so eager to pursue them; why can't we be as hungry to find use in our lives for a Christlike spirit of love?

Wilberforce's prediction proved to be on the mark. From the time of Pitt's arrival in the House of Commons, he made a positive impression. He delivered an excellent first speech in the Commons on financial reform. Many agreed with Wilberforce's assessment that Pitt would soon be a contender for prime minister. Later Pitt speeches criticizing the government for its handling of the war in the colonies won additional acclaim. Wilberforce, meanwhile, lacked passion and had identified no major causes to address in his early days in Commons. He first spoke during the debate on a bill to control smuggling and next entered the debate on naval shipbuilding. Neither effort earned him a place in history. More important, he used his early years in Commons to build relationships with other members, to become familiar with legislative procedures, and to analyze the persuasive styles of the more effective members.

Wilberforce at first took his place with the Tories, the party of William Pitt. The Tories were associated with the effort to reform Parliament and were connected with business interests more than their rivals, the Whigs, who were more often the aristocrats. In reality, the parties were far less important than they would be later, and Wilberforce was more loyal to Pitt than to the party.

One of Wilberforce's major challenges during the years he represented Hull was gaining acceptance into the social networks of London. Ironically, his background as a member of a merchant and banking family was a liability in that regard. He had plenty of money but not the social standing enjoyed by the aristocracy. He set out to gain acceptance through the same assets that had made him popular at Cambridge—his wealth, wit, an impressive speaking voice, and, at times, his singing ability. In this process of building social relationships in national life, there was almost no substitute for actively participating in one or more of the members-only social clubs. That was where one forged friendships and established relationships of trust. Social clubs were also where one could soften the opposition of those who might block one's efforts, and where signals could be cleared and plans developed.

Two of the clubs were identified with the two major parties. The Tories tended to congregate at White's, while the Whigs favored Brookes's. Wilberforce joined both so he would be able to gain support from either party. Not needing to watch his

WILLIAM WILBERFORCE ON APPROVAL

If we find that we are well-liked and popular, then we should think that we have got more than we bargained for—and then watch ourselves all the more carefully for fear we become too fond of something that we will soon be asked to give up. We need to consider often that worldly fame never lasts; we may all have to submit ourselves sooner or later to disgrace and criticism, so we should become comfortable with its face, so that we are not taken by surprise. We need to cultivate in our hearts the desire for "that honour which cometh from God," for this is the most effective means of bringing our thoughts into perspective in regards to the love of human approval.

pennies, he also joined Boodle's, Miles and Evans, and Goosetree's. The clubs helped Wilberforce form alliances for future battles. As a young single man, he essentially made the clubs his home, a place to pass the time pleasantly when not involved in the duties of office. For some club members the attraction was gambling. While Wilberforce did his share of that, he decided to abstain from the compulsive gambling that financially ruined some club members.

After four years, Wilberforce was beginning to get a feel for how things got done in the Parliament. Even though he had worked with Pitt on some major projects, he didn't feel he had much to show for his four years of effort. He had strong support in Hull, but simply staying in office was not exactly a worthy goal in life. He knew a lot of people but felt he ought to be doing more than building friendships.

A trip to France, though, showed that both young politicians had much to learn.

"Pitt, you did take care of obtaining a letter of introduction to the French officials in Rheims, didn't you?"

"I thought you were going to do that," replied Pitt.

Their traveling companion and friend, Edward Eliot, thought the situation extremely funny as they traveled across the English Channel with no idea how they would make connections in the French government. Once on French soil, the three found adequate lodging, and Pitt proceeded to find someone willing to write the appropriate letter introducing them as well-placed English visitors who should be extended every courtesy while visiting France.

Providentially, when the Abbe de Lageard, the ranking official at Rheims, was informed that the introduction Pitt had scrambled to find came from a Monseiur Coustier, a shopkeeper who could get them into the local wholesalers but not much more, he took the three young men under his wing. During their stay in Paris, they were able to meet with the Marquis de Lafayette and Benjamin Franklin, and they were even granted an audience with Queen Marie Antoinette. At the palace, news of the foreign travelers' difficulty in obtaining a viable introduction had clearly preceded them.

"I've been curious to meet you three young Englishmen," the queen remarked. "What is this I hear about your excellent connections here in France? Is it true that you actually had a letter from a neighborhood grocer?" She paused long enough to make Pitt, Wilberforce, and Eliot feel the full weight of their faux pas. "Do not worry, my young friends. You are most welcome in our country. We will show you we are not quite the barbarians you think we are."

Little did the doomed queen realize she was in the company of a future world leader—and one whose conscience would change the world.

> "You did not choose me, but I chose you and appointed you to go and bear fruit—fruit that will last. Then the Father will give you whatever you ask in my name."
>
> JOHN 15:16 NIV

4

A WHALE OF A MAN

Wilberforce was delighted when word went out that the king might soon appoint William Pitt prime minister. He believed Pitt was deserving of the honor, and although he would be the youngest prime minister ever, he certainly would not be the least qualified. Many in the House of Commons agreed with Wilberforce's opinion and promised their support.

Pitt would need all the friends he could find. Wilberforce was a gifted speaker, and every ounce of his wit would be needed to carry the day on some of the close votes to come. Pitt also needed trusted friends like Wilberforce for consultation and strategizing.

For himself, Wilberforce had no major goals in Parliament other than representing Hull well. He valued Pitt's friendship and supported his goals for reform in Parliament. He also shared Pitt's distaste for the way the war in America was handled—but he expected no rewards from him for his support, apart from his respect and loyalty. Someday Wilberforce might aspire to a stronger seat in the House and set about to address some major issues, but for now he was content to be Pitt's friend.

As he bumped along on the road to York to attend a political rally, William couldn't help but think how Pitt might be helpful to him in the future. He probably could ask for some sort of position in the new government, since he would be one of Pitt's backers and Pitt would probably win the election. Wilberforce knew he would not be given one of the major ministry posts, since he represented a relatively minor borough. And he didn't really want to be given an appointment, in any case. There seemed to be something more important in his future, though he didn't know what.

The meeting in York had been called by the Yorkshire Association, a reform group formed a few years before. Wilberforce had a slight acquaintance with the head of this group, Christopher Wyvill, a clergyman with an estate and some political influence.

Wilberforce knew that the Yorkshire Association hoped to gain support at the meeting for sending a message to the king asking for a new election. These reformers who would give their support to the reform goals of William Pitt hoped to identify potential members of Parliament from Yorkshire who would back Pitt and his reform agenda.

Apart from giving support to Pitt at the rally, Wilberforce began thinking about a way he could help Pitt even more. Wouldn't it be good for Pitt and for himself if he were to come away from the York meeting as one of the two candidates from Yorkshire in the next elections?

Wilberforce had shown above-average skill at the gambling tables that were common pastimes for those of his position, but the odds of going from an obscure MP from Hull to one of the two members from Yorkshire almost made him laugh out loud. It was not a new idea to him, but he hadn't even had the courage to mention this to his friend Pitt. There were twenty thousand electors in Yorkshire, almost twenty times the number of voters in Hull. In fact, these two Yorkshire seats had more constituent power than any in the House of Commons.

In Hull, Wilberforce had benefited from the name

recognition of his wealthy merchant family, but in Yorkshire there was strong preference in politics for those among the landed aristocracy. There were growing industrial cities such as Sheffield, Leeds, Halifax, and Bradford in Yorkshire, but those involved in industry were no match politically for the landed class. Land and titles were of far greater consequence in the British caste structure of the eighteenth century than the "new wealth" of the merchant class.

Wilberforce knew that he could not repeat the tactics in Yorkshire that had gained him a seat in Hull. There he followed the common practice of providing payments to those who supported him. There he could travel about the entire borough, talking with electors and winning their confidence. Yorkshire was far too large to meet all of the voters, and there was little time before the election. Moreover, the cost of providing payments averaging eight pounds per voter would be far more than he could afford.

In fact, elections had rarely been held in Yorkshire in the eighteenth century. Because campaigning was so costly, the backers of particular candidates organized canvasses, systematically making contact with voters in various areas. These canvasses were the equivalent of modern opinion polls and were just as accurate. Within weeks the backers of candidates could gather evidence of the amount of support their candidates had and, if successful, convince opponents that it would be futile to ask for an election.

As his carriage took him closer to York, Wilberforce weighed the practicality of becoming a candidate from Yorkshire. A long shot? Indeed, it was like betting on a horse that had come in last ten races in a row. More than being little known in the county and from the wrong social and economic class, he was aware that there were two incumbents fully intending to win out in the canvassing process. Francis Foljambe,

WILLIAM WILBERFORCE ON SELF-KNOWLEDGE

Scrutinize yourself rigorously. If you think you have a blind spot, then ask for help from some faithful friend. Be completely honest and ask for an impartial and unreserved opinion of your behavior and condition. Our unwillingness to do this often betrays to others as it reveals to ourselves that we have a secret distrust of our own character and conduct.

one of the incumbents, was the nephew of Sir George Savile, who had held the seat for more than twenty years. Foljambe had the backing of both the Yorkshire Association and the powerful landed families. Yorkshire's other member, Henry Duncombe, had gained his seat in 1780 through the specific efforts of the association members.

Once there, Wilberforce was warmly greeted by William Mason, his host, who was also from Hull.

"Could you give me a briefing on the alignment of political forces at tomorrow's meeting? In London we don't hear much about political events in places like Yorkshire."

Mason nodded his head. "Better yet, the association's head, Christopher Wyvill, is to be our guest for high tea, and he can give you a better explanation than I. But let me give you a bit of information."

In sotto voce, Mason began to describe the situation. The main question was whether the voters at the meeting would support a request to the king to dissolve Parliament and call an election. The even more important issues were who would gain support as new members and how they would align on their backing of Charles Fox and the coalition on the one hand and William Pitt and his new government on the other.

Mason was a backer of Pitt, which meant he would support Duncombe's reelection. Fulcombe was officially in support of reform, but he made no secret of his preference for Fox, as did his major backers, Lord Fitzwilliam and the most powerful landed families.

"Mason, I agree with everything you've said so far. I've supported Pitt in these last few months in the Commons. I've known him since our days at Cambridge, and I have the highest regard for his ability and his integrity. In fact, I came here specifically to do what I could to support efforts that might gain him backing from Yorkshire in forming a new government.

"But if you don't mind my saying so, the weather here in York is horrible. How do you expect a decent showing at the meeting tomorrow? It's to be held outdoors on the castle grounds, yes? I'd be shocked if we get more than a handful of voters."

"Oh, they will come, Wilberforce. I've seen the carriages coming to town for several days, and most of the inns are full. You've heard the phrase 'idle rich,' right? What better do the leaders of the county have to do in March than see their friends and choose sides in a major political fight? The speeches will be boring, of course, but there's a lot at stake. You'll be amazed when you see the crowd tomorrow. I'll wager that it will be in the thousands."

Mason's prediction was on the mark. Four thousand voters assembled on the castle grounds on March 25, in spite of a mix of cold wind, hail, and rain. There was a covered platform for the speakers, but the crowd had to endure the bitter conditions without protection. Speaker after speaker held forth, expressing their support of or opposition to William Pitt's plans for a new reform government. Duncombe spoke in support of Pitt, while his fellow incumbent, Foljambe, declined to speak, sensing the crowd would not be friendly to his pro-Fox sentiments.

As head of the sponsoring group, Christopher Wyvill controlled access to the platform. The previous evening at William Mason's house, he had gratefully accepted the help of William Wilberforce in preparing his remarks for the day. Seeing Wilberforce near the platform in midafternoon, Wyvill beckoned to him and offered him a place in the roster of speakers. He warned Wilberforce that the crowd was tired and cold and suggested he make it short and forceful and be sure he could be heard over the wind.

While waiting for his turn on the platform, Wilberforce wondered if he should have accepted

Wyvill's invitation to speak. Who was he to try making an impression among this array of impressive speakers? What could he say that hadn't already been said? What hope did he have that the crowd wouldn't all head immediately to the warmth of the nearest pub when he took the stand?

"Mr. Wilberforce made a most argumentative and eloquent speech, which was listened to with the most eager attention, and received with the loudest acclamations of applause," said the newspaper report of William's speech. "There was such an exquisite choice of expression, and pronounced with such rapidity, that we are unable to do it justice in any account we can give of it," continued the story.

Wilberforce used his knowledge of the India Bill to attack its sponsors, headed by Charles Fox, and to support its opponents, led by William Pitt. He cautioned the powerful landholders in the crowd that legislation like the India Bill could lead to future actions undermining their freedoms. James Boswell, the Scottish biographer of Samuel Johnson, said that he first thought he was listening to a shrimp of a man, but soon concluded that this was no shrimp, but a whale.[5]

The speech might have ended and the rally

concluded with no direct benefit to Wilberforce had it not been for a helpful turn of events. After speaking for about an hour and realizing he needed to conclude soon, Wilberforce saw a rustle of activity on the edge of the crowd. Was it a group of people getting ready to leave? No, it was a rider in a great hurry. As the man made his way through the crowd, it was apparent from his appearance that he was a messenger from the king. Accurately guessing the content of the message, Wilberforce beckoned the man forward and asked if he might read the message to the crowd. The note was from Pitt to Wilberforce, dated at noon the day before. It reported that Parliament had been dissolved.

Wilberforce, a master of extemporaneous speaking, used the opportunity to declare that the immediate goals of the day's gathering had been reached. The long-range goals would be achieved only if those present would declare their firm support for William Pitt in the coming election.

Wilberforce's speech did much for Pitt's cause, but it did even more to further Wilberforce's own ambitions. In his note, Pitt urged Wilberforce to do his best to gain support for their mutual reform goals, a tacit endorsement for Wilberforce, whom

Pitt could not have known would be on the platform at the time. Some members of the crowd got the point and called out that they wanted Wilberforce as one of their county's members. This must have seemed ludicrous to those who had never heard of the man an hour before, but all were impressed with him and only the Fox supporters were brave enough to question the idea of Wilberforce as a county candidate. The meeting ended with an endorsement of the king's action in dissolving Parliament but no agreement on how the voters would proceed to select their two members.

Supporters of Fox and Pitt selected different places to caucus over dinner and drinks. When the Pitt people gathered at York Tavern, it turned out that support for Pitt was one of the few things on which the caucus could agree. They had many arguments during the evening, and heavy drinking added to the ill will. Wilberforce used the support he had gained that afternoon to assist Wyvill in making peace among the angry factions at the dinner. For his efforts, Wilberforce gained the acclamation of some of the Pitt supporters for his candidacy as one of Yorkshire's members. As the meeting broke up, supporters of Wilberforce cried out that they would support his candidacy.

The next day another gathering of Pitt supporters agreed to back Duncombe and Wilberforce as their candidates, rejecting a proposal from the Fox group that Duncombe and Foljambe be retained in office. Knowing that even a canvass would be expensive and the cost of an election would be prohibitive, Pitt and Wilberforce supporters pledged ten thousand pounds to pursue the campaign.

With growing support but no guarantee of the outcome, Wilberforce had to go back to Hull to campaign for his present seat. He accomplished that successfully, in spite of some resentment over his effort to gain the more prestigious position representing Yorkshire.

Less than two weeks after the rally in York, Wilberforce not only won the Hull seat but participated energetically in the canvassing of Yorkshire. Wyvill was able to mobilize a network of local Yorkshire Association committees on behalf of the Duncombe/ Wilberforce ticket. The canvass showed that the two Pitt candidates had four times the support of the Fox candidates, Foljambe and William Weddell.

WILLIAM WILBERFORCE ON SPIRITUAL GIFTS

Beat the world with its own best weapons. Let your love be more gentle, your gentleness less vulnerable to irritation, your diligence more hardworking, your activity more alert and persevering. Examine yourself. If you see that a gentle temperament or an energetic constitution belong naturally to your character, then consider these qualities as you would if they were talents of special worth and usefulness. Remember, you are accountable for these gifts. Be careful not to let anything hurt these natural qualities; take care of them constantly, and direct them to their noblest goals.

The rest was anticlimactic. The Fox backers withdrew, and one of their leaders grumbled about their defeat by ragamuffins like Wilberforce who were not part of the aristocracy.

Wilberforce's cryptic diary entry understated his amazement and happiness at the surprising victory. He wrote, "Up early—breakfasted tavern—rode frisky horse to castle—elected—chaired—dined York Tavern."

His friend William Pitt understood the significance of the victory and its implications for both of them. Pitt wrote, "I can never enough congratulate you on such a glorious success."[6] In a few days' time, Wilberforce had gone from a relatively weak position in Parliament to one of its most powerful seats. He had created a base from which he might undertake almost any cause in the future.

First, though, there was the matter of his soul. For whom would William Wilberforce really serve. . .and to what would his life be a testament?

> Blessed is he whose help is the God of Jacob, whose hope is in the LORD his God.
>
> PSALM 146:5 NIV

5

AWAKENING

The two carriages sped along the rutted road to Dover, one carrying two well-dressed gentlemen and the other, a bevy of gowns and hats.

"Milner, I can't thank you enough for joining us on the trip to France," Wilberforce said, his voice conveying relief. He would have preferred to vacation in England, but his mother, his sister Sally, and two female cousins were determined to visit France, and he was stuck with accompanying them.

"How could I argue with the chance to get away from Cambridge? But tell the truth: I suppose you needed an excuse not to ride in the carriage with the women, correct?"

"Yes, but you won't quote me on that, will you?"

Wilberforce had had some difficulty finding someone to join him on the trip to and from France. A fortunate meeting with Isaac Milner in Scarborough had prompted him to invite the professor to join the expedition. At least they could talk about their days at Hull School and Cambridge, where Milner had led the class in mathematics. Wilberforce knew there was a lot he could learn from Milner. He was a little bothered that Milner's brother, Joseph, had become an evangelical, but his traveling companion had assured him he was not about to try to convert anyone.

Wilberforce, perhaps unconsciously, was well on the way to a more fulfilling spiritual life. He professed having a favorable impression of Theophilus Lindsey, a preacher who had concluded that much of the New Testament material was added by early followers of Christ who made Him into the sort of divine being He never presented himself to be. Lindsey said the stories of the miracles and healings and even the resurrection were added to the Gospels by people who got carried away with their admiration for Christ. Lindsey believed in God and the scriptures, but he concentrated on the parts of the Bible that were most consistent with the reasoning of modern man. He called himself a Unitarian, based on the understanding that God is one being, not three separate persons.

Milner had heard about Lindsey, but as he told Wilberforce, he wouldn't go far out of his way to hear him preach. Milner believed the Bible to be God's inspired and authoritative message. He freely admitted that he could not explain the entire book, but simply because he couldn't understand something in the Bible didn't make it untrue. He admitted that there was much in his life that didn't square with the evangelical life, but where it matters most— in his understanding of and commitment to Jesus as Savior and Lord of his life—he could be called an evangelical.

Milner and Wilberforce agreed to disagree, spending their time discussing other matters.

After the party had spent some weeks in France, Pitt wrote to Wilberforce, urging him to return for the introduction of a parliamentary reform bill. Wilberforce, who had no great love for French food and culture, was happy for an excuse to return. Before departing, he noticed a book owned by his cousin Bessy Smith—Philip Doddridge's *The Rise and Progress of*

WILLIAM WILBERFORCE ON GROWTH IN GRACE

In order to grow in grace, we must study at the same school. All the practical wisdom we need, an inexhaustible store-house of instructions and inspiration, are to be found in the gospel, by contemplating the life and character and suffer-ings of our blessed Savior. Neglecting to do this will give rise to some of the most common practical errors that are com-mitted by those who merely profess to be Christians. If we keep these gigantic truths always in view, they put to shame our own dwarfish little concepts of morality.

Religion in the Soul. Doddridge, who had died several decades before, was something of a spiritual father to Whitefield and Wesley in his emphasis on salvation by faith in Christ. The well-written book was standard fare among evangelicals of the day.

Wondering if the book would help pass the long hours on the trip back to England, Wilberforce asked Milner if it would be worth reading. Milner knew the book and endorsed it enthusiastically. He suggested they read and discuss it together on the return trip.

Doddridge's views didn't square well with those of Reverend Lindsey, and Wilberforce wasn't sure whom he found more believable. While Doddridge wouldn't fare too well in the theology debates at Cambridge, there was something about the directness of his reasoning that Wilberforce liked. Lindsey had a way of picking and choosing parts of the Bible that suited him, content to set aside any passage that couldn't be worked out through human reasoning.

"It's sort of like worshiping part of God and ignoring the other parts of Him, don't you think?" he asked Milner.

"I think we must accept by faith the key elements of the gospel, such as the divinity of Jesus, the inspiration of the scriptures, Christ's resurrection, and the need for repentance and conversion," Milner responded. "Do I understand all of that? No, but I believe it. And I trust a loving God to reveal as much of the truth of the gospel as is important for us to understand."

Before making the return trip to France, Wilberforce found there was plenty of work for him to do in Commons, in addition to keeping his constituents happy. He and Pitt had written and introduced a new bill on parliamentary reform, but it would be another matter to get it approved. The bill would eliminate thirty-five of the many "rotten" boroughs, but those who had profited from the system were understandably upset.

Pitt was in an awkward spot. He was the number one champion of reform in the country, but he had entered Parliament from a rotten borough himself after losing his campaign in Cambridge. Fortunately, Wilberforce didn't have that problem.

Despite his conversations with Milner, Wilberforce still spent his free hours singing, drinking, and dancing. His frail body was not up to that sort of life anymore, and he needed a holiday after only four months back at work. He was almost glad when it was time to head back to France to escort his family home. He and Milner were able to resume their conversations about theology, both during the trip and in France.

"William, we've hardly seen you during this trip," Wilberforce's mother complained. "What on earth do you talk about with Isaac Milner for hour after hour? Can't you spend a little time with us?"

"I'm sorry, Mother. I must say I'm rather surprised at myself. Believe it or not, I hunted up my copy of the Greek New Testament before this trip, and we have been reading it along the way, talking about some of the difficult passages."

"You know very well that religious fanaticism will not be acceptable to your constituents," Elizabeth replied brusquely. "You also know that many of the Methodists completely cut themselves off from the life of our social groups. They don't go to the opera and theater and don't dine out very often. You could throw away your entire career and all the good things you might do if you turn your back on our way of life and the teaching of the Church of England."

William took a deep breath and exhaled slowly. "Mother, I love you and my sister very much and I don't want to disappoint you, but I must follow my heart and my mind. So far my views on religion haven't affected my daily life much at all, and no one in politics would have any reason to call me a religious fanatic. I can only say I have come to believe in Christ as my Savior and Lord, and I don't think that will take me away from the Church of England. It may actually take me back to the most important things at the heart of the church."

The changes in Wilberforce's inner life had been steady and dramatic, and soon the inner changes

WILLIAM WILBERFORCE ON FAILURE

Every now and then, get in the habit of looking at the terrible consequences of failure—and then fix your attention on the glorious prize that lies ahead of you if you succeed. When your strength begins to fail and your spirits are almost exhausted, let this life-giving view rekindle your resolution, calling forth a renewed vigor in your soul.

began to affect his outward life. While still in Europe with his family, he took some small but significant steps toward what he felt was a godlier style of living. He began to abstain from some activities on Sundays, such as attending the opera and theater. He then began to arise early each day for prayer and meditation and soon after that began keeping a daily spiritual journal. Those times of personal reflection led to enormous inner turmoil before he reached a point of spiritual equilibrium. He later wrote the following:

> *As soon as I reflected seriously, the deep guilt and black ingratitude of my past life forced itself on me in the strongest colours, and I condemned*

myself for having wasted precious time, and op-
portunities and talents. . . . It was not so much
the fear of punishment by which I was affected,
as a sense of my great sinfulness in having so
long neglected the unspeakable mercies of my
God and Savior; and such was the effect which
this thought produced, that for months I was
in a state of the deepest depression, from strong
convictions of my guilt. Indeed nothing which I
have ever read in the accounts of others exceeded
what I then felt.[7]

Clearly, Wilberforce was experiencing a spiritual
struggle, one common to all Christians once they
examine their past lives—and then reflect on the
blessings of their Savior. His dilemma, though, was
slightly different: Could he take his newfound faith
seriously without abandoning his career in Parliament?

> It is God who works in you to will and to
> act according to his good purpose.
>
> PHILIPPIANS 2:13 NIV

6

THE BATTLE WITH PRIDE

In late 1785, William sat at his desk, struggling with the wording of a letter to the prime minister of England, William Pitt. Wilberforce's association with Pitt had been crucial in his election as a member from Yorkshire. In turn, Wilberforce's efforts to promote Pitt's reform agenda in that election had been central to solidifying Pitt's political base in Parliament.

As he thought about what to say to Pitt, Wilberforce looked at some of the entries in his journal. The intensity of his new spiritual commitment and the turmoil he felt about what this might mean in his life, personally and politically, were revealed in these words:

I must awake to my dangerous state, and never be at rest till I have made peace with God. My heart is so hard, my blindness so great, that I cannot get a due hatred of sin, though I see I am all corrupt, and blinded to the perception of spiritual things.

True, Lord, I am wretched, and miserable, and blind, and naked. What infinite love, that Christ should die to save such a sinner, and how necessary is it He should save us altogether, that we may appear before God with nothing of our own!

Pride is my greatest stumbling block; and there is danger in it in two ways—lest it should make me desist from a Christian life, through fear of the world, my friends, etc; or if I persevere, lest it should make me vain of so doing.

O God, give me a heart of flesh! Nothing so convinces me of the dreadful state of my own mind as the possibility, which, if I did not know if from experience, I should believe impossible, of my being ashamed of Christ. Ashamed of the Creator of all things! One who has received infinite pardon and mercy, ashamed of the Dispenser of it, and that in a country where his name is professed! Oh, what should I have done in persecuting times?[28]

Wilberforce thought about the time that week he had spent with Pitt—and he felt ashamed that he had not talked about his new faith in Christ. He knew he could not wait for the perfect chance to talk. He would write his feelings on paper.

In the letter, Wilberforce determined to tell Pitt about his newfound faith in Christ and also to address the possibility that he might have to abandon

WORLD EVENTS OF 1785

The United States adopts the dollar—the first decimal-based system—as its unit of currency.

The London newspaper *The Daily Universal Register*—later known as *The Times*—begins publication.

The University of Georgia is founded.

Frenchman Jean-Pierre Blanchard and American John Jeffries cross the English Channel in a hydrogen balloon.

Coal gas is first used for illumination.

his promising career in politics, if this was what it might require to be faithful in following Christ. At the very least, he would have to set aside many aspects of the social life that had been part of his life from his university days. He also told Pitt he would no longer be a "party man" in a different sense. If he were to stay in politics, he would no longer be free to support his allies and friends in Parliament at all times but would find it necessary to follow his own moral and spiritual convictions, whatever those might be. Wilberforce ended the letter by expressing his hope that their

WILLIAM WILBERFORCE ON PATRIOTISM

If we define patriotism as the dangerous and domineering tendency to promote not the nation's well-being, but its glory at the cost of other nations, a tendency that leads to oppression and conquest, then we would have to say that Christianity is an enemy of patriotism. But if we understand patriotism to give us a love for our own land, a love that never confines our concern for humanity to our political boundaries, then Christianity gives abundant encouragement to this brand of patriotic feeling.

friendship might remain intact, even though they might have to relate to one another differently. Rather than take the risk that their differences in moral and spiritual values might adversely affect their friendship, Wilberforce asked that they not even talk of these matters further.

The reply from Prime Minister Pitt arrived quickly, and Wilberforce read it with a good bit of anxiety. "You will not suspect me of thinking lightly of any moral or religious motives which guide you. But forgive me if I cannot help expressing my fear that you are deluding yourself into principles which have but too much tendency to counteract your own object, and to render your virtues and your talents useless both to yourself and to mankind." Pitt went on to directly challenge Wilberforce's notion that faithfulness to Christ might require him to leave his career in politics. "If a Christian may act in the several relations of life, must he seclude himself from all to become so? Surely the principles as well as the practice of Christianity are simple, and lead not to meditation only, but to action."

Wilberforce had suggested that the two might no longer be close friends if their values were substantially different. Pitt questioned the need for Wilberforce's spiritual zeal to create a rift between them:

As to any public conduct which your opinion may ever lead you to, I will not disguise to you that few things could go nearer my heart than to find myself differing from you on any great principle. I trust and believe that it is a circumstance that can hardly occur. . . . Believe me it is impossible that it should shake the sentiments of affection and friendship which I bear towards you, and which I must be forgetful and insensible indeed if I ever could part with. They are sentiments engraved on my heart and will never be effaced or weakened.[9]

Not content to let the exchange of letters bring their discussion to an end, Prime Minister Pitt went out of his way the following day to call on Wilberforce at Wimbledon. The discussion was long and intense. Pitt assured Wilberforce that their friendship was too important to both of them to be threatened by their differing views of religion.

> What good is it, my brothers, if a man claims to have faith but has no deeds? Can such faith save him?
> JAMES 2:14 NIV

Pitt considered himself a Christian and a faithful member of the church. He admitted Wilberforce's courage in putting his faith ahead of everything else, but begged him not to throw away all he could accomplish in his life through politics. Pitt was sure that one of these days Wilberforce would find a cause that would ignite his talents and energies. "Can you not serve your God while in politics, instead of heading off into some sort of monastic life?" he asked.

Wilberforce replied that perhaps God would open a way for him to stay in public life while still being obedient to His directions, but either way, he had to be faithful to God's leading.

Pitt was not ready to follow Wilberforce's spiritual leadership, but he hoped that he could count on his friend to keep his seat from Yorkshire and back his causes in the House whenever he could. He would try to understand if Wilberforce felt he must oppose him on some points and asked that Wilberforce respect him when he took a position that Wilberforce could not support.

"Amazing grace! How sweet the sound, that saved a wretch like me! I once was lost, but now am found, was blind but now I see."

The words of the hymn "Amazing Grace" may have been going through Wilberforce's head as he walked around the block where the hymn's author, John Newton, lived. The entries in Wilberforce's journal at the time expressed the same sentiments as the hymn: the great joy in deliverance from spiritual blindness and wretchedness.

The author of the hymn was the same John Newton whom Wilberforce had heard preach when he was a boy—and who was part of the spiritual environment from which his mother had abruptly removed him. And this was the same John Newton who had been delivered from his own lifestyle as a sea captain and the institutional evil in which he had participated for years, the slave trade. Newton had since responded to a call to the ministry in the Church of England, and he was supportive of the growing evangelical movement inside and outside the church.

The following lines from another of Newton's hymns, "How Sweet the Name of Jesus Sounds," may also have been comforting Wilberforce as he walked around the block in Newton's parish, St. Mary Woolnoth, a second time: "It makes the wounded spirit whole, and calms the troubled breast;

'tis manna to the hungry soul, and to the weary, rest; and to the weary, rest."

Certainly Wilberforce was ready for some rest from his struggles to be faithful to the leading of the Holy Spirit. The letter to William Pitt and subsequent conversation had brought some emotional relief, but he couldn't get away from the conviction that he was supposed to go see John Newton. In his journal he had argued with himself about it. He knew it would be helpful to establish contact with the pastor whose sermons he had valued as a boy. Could it be that Pitt was selfishly urging him to stay in politics? Could it be that someone like Newton, without a vested interest in politics, would counsel him to make a clean break from his present life and follow God's leading in a different direction?

In his journal Wilberforce had correctly named the source of his hesitation about meeting with Newton. It was spiritual pride that was stopping Wilberforce from going ahead to meet Newton, a lowly preacher, far below Wilberforce in social standing. More to the point, Newton was one of the despised "Methodists," those who had experienced the kind of conversion that was emphasized so much by John Wesley and the other evangelicals. There was no Methodist denomination at the time, but those who believed in and practiced the emphasis on conversion and forgiveness from sins were all labeled Methodists and were viewed with derision, reflecting the sentiments of Wilberforce's mother.

WILLIAM WILBERFORCE ON PRIDE

In the Bible we learn the painful lesson of human degradation and unworthiness. We learn that humility and contrition are the emotions best suited to our fallen condition and most acceptable in the sight of our Creator. In addition, we learn that we should habitually cherish and cultivate these feelings, while we put off our arrogance and self-importance. We are to studiously maintain a continual sense that any natural advantages we may have over others mean nothing in God's eyes; instead, His love for us depends totally on His own unmerited mercy.

Even though Wilberforce walked around Newton's house, he could not summon the courage to go knock on the door. Instead, he wrote a letter to Newton proposing that they meet. So afraid was Wilberforce that someone would learn of their correspondence that he tore his signature from the letter and urged Newton not to tell anyone they had been in touch.

Wilberforce knew his Bible well and might have thought about the Old Testament account of Naaman, an army commander who was directed by the prophet Elisha to wash in the Jordan River in order to receive God's healing from leprosy. What could be simpler? But from Naaman's point of view, what could be more humiliating than to wash in the Jordan, not nearly as impressive as the rivers back in Naaman's hometown of Damascus? For Wilberforce, going to visit John Newton was like washing in the Jordan River. It meant humbling himself and taking the risk of being identified with one of the better-known evangelical clergymen of the day.

At last, Wilberforce's determination to follow Christ at any cost won out over his fear and pride, and he kept an appointment with Newton. One of Wilberforce's fears was that Newton would counsel him to leave his career in politics to be completely obedient to Christ. After all, Newton had left his work as a ship captain after his conversion. But this was not the counsel Newton gave Wilberforce. "The Lord has raised you up for the good of his church and for the good of his nation," declared Newton, echoing the point made a few days before by Pitt.

"The very fact of your being obedient today is probably of more consequence than anything that has transpired today," Newton said. He believed Wilberforce had much to offer the work of God's kingdom. He didn't want Wilberforce to do anything but follow God's leading, whether that meant staying in Parliament or leaving. That said, Newton believed God had some great work ahead for Wilberforce.

Humble yourselves, therefore, under God's mighty hand, that he may lift you up in due time. Cast all your anxiety on him because he cares for you.

1 PETER 5: 6–7 NIV

7

HIGHER PURPOSE

T he first years I was in Parliament, I did nothing—nothing, that is, to any purpose. My own distinction was my darling object." This was the way William Wilberforce assessed his first two years representing Yorkshire in Parliament. Was he too hard on himself? Yes, but at the time he was introspective and unhappy, feeling that there was some higher purpose for his life now that he had fully surrendered to Christ.

But it was true that Wilberforce did not accomplish much of lasting consequence in public life in 1786 and 1787, other than becoming familiar with the procedures and the culture of the House of Commons. One of his first initiatives had a noble aim—parliamentary reform—but after Wilberforce

WORLD EVENTS OF 1787

The United States Constitution is adopted by the Constitutional Convention in Philadelphia.

Delaware, Pennsylvania, and New Jersey, respectively, become the first three states.

German-born British astronomer William Herschel discovers two moons of Uranus.

Rev. Thomas Hopkins Gallaudet, pioneer in education for the deaf, is born in Philadelphia.

became more familiar with the particular bill he had supported, he was relieved that it failed to pass the House of Lords. The bill would have required voter registration to occur in one place and on one day in the member's district. On further reflection, it appeared that this restriction would hinder voter participation, particularly in a large jurisdiction like Yorkshire.[10]

Wilberforce's other early attempt at legislative work also failed and helped him realize that public policy issues were far more complex than they first appeared. Again, the cause was noble—reform of the criminal justice system. But the remedy proved to be problematic. Parliamentary measures in that day were wordy and obtuse, at least for modern tastes. Consider Wilberforce's bill, which was titled "A Bill for Regulating the Disposal after Execution of the Bodies of Criminals Executed for Certain Offences, and for Changing the Sentence Pronounced Upon Female Convicts in Certain Cases of High and Petty Treason."[11]

Wilberforce's bill would have outlawed a practice he and his supporters considered to be brutal and inappropriate, the burning or dissection of the bodies of convicted criminals once they were hanged. Opponents of his measure saw the practice as a deterrent against crime, but Wilberforce despised such spectacles. One hanging and burning that year had attracted twenty thousand spectators to Newgate prison. But banning dissection of these bodies would have had the unintended effect of hindering scientific research and medical training, leaving it to body snatchers to provide cadavers for those legitimate purposes. In any event, the House of Lords defeated the bill, its spokesman calling it "ill-advised and impracticable."

WILLIAM WILBERFORCE ON FOCUS

God will not accept from us a love that is divided by selfishness; He wants from us both singleness of heart and an attention that is whole and undistracted. The Bible tells us that we amass heavenly treasure if we make the favor and service of God our chief pursuit, for "where our treasure is, there will our hearts be also." This is why the Bible condemns various vices—not because they are innately wrong in and of themselves, but because they draw our hearts away from Him whom we should prefer over all else.

Wilberforce struggled to find a comfortable place for himself socially as well as politically, in view of his new spiritual commitments. He continued to withdraw from many of his previous social involvements, feeling they were contrary to his convictions as a serious follower of Christ. He resigned from a number of the social clubs in which he had been active and which were considered to be both the privilege and the duty of members of Parliament. He stopped gambling, which had been a centerpiece of his socializing earlier, and he stopped going to dances and the theater.

As a politician of growing prominence, Wilberforce was expected to appear at major events in the county he represented, such as horse races, balls, and dinners. While knowing his absence from these events might hurt him politically, he no longer enjoyed the frivolity of upper-class social life. Typical of the uncertainty he felt about the social choices he was making was his comment to his political ally Christopher Wyvill that his constituents might misunderstand his lack of participation in social events. He wondered if his behavior would "excite disgust rather than cordiality." Wyvill encouraged him to chart his own course rather than violate his convictions and priorities.[12]

In place of the social whirl that had filled Wilberforce's younger years, he set about to make up for his lack of diligence in his studies at Cambridge. During an extended stay with friends near Nottingham, he maintained a daily routine that included up to ten hours a day of studying history, economics, literature, philosophy, and science. He limited his social time with his hosts and their guests so he could spend ample time with the ideas of the great thinkers he had neglected at the university: Montesquieu, Adam Smith, Blackstone, Locke, Pope, and Johnson. At the same time, Wilberforce included careful study of the Bible among his new disciplines. His cousin Henry Thornton said of the "new Wilberforce" at this time, "His enlarged mind, his affectionate and understanding manners and his very superior piety were exactly calculated to supply what was wanting to my improvement and my establishment in the right course."[13]

The changes in Wilberforce's life during 1786, as he engaged in serious study and reduced his social activities, prepared him to give greater attention to his purpose in life. He continued to be unsure where he should devote his energies in the Parliament. Although he had decided that God would have him continue to pursue politics as a vocation, he did not know whether there was some particular moral or spiritual cause he should pursue. During this time of seeking direction, seeds began to be planted for what became his best-known life accomplishment, the abolition of the slave trade.

WILLIAM WILBERFORCE ON LEGALISM

One of the saddest consequences of seeing Christianity as a collection of laws and not as an internal principle, is that soon we base our faith on a set of external actions, rather than on habits of the mind. This false way of thinking can worm its way into our minds under the guise of concern for practical faith. Soon, though, it reveals the falsehood behind this thinking, betraying its real nature. It makes as much sense to put all our effort into external behavior while we pay no attention at all to the internal principles from which our actions flow as it would for an architect to say that we should save our money by not laying any foundation, so that we could use it all for raising the superstructure. We know what would happen to a building that was built like that!

The Portuguese first transported slaves to Europe for sale in 1444. For fifty years the slaves were put to work only in Portugal and the volume of the trade was modest. In 1503 the Portuguese first took slaves to the New World colonies and in a few years began direct shipment from Africa to America.

English traders did not participate in the early years of this trade, and furthermore, English opinion did not favor this type of trade. But when England began to acquire colonies in the Caribbean and North America, slaves became a solution for the needed manual labor of plantation agriculture. Moreover, English merchants and shippers began to see the potential for lucrative gains in the three-way trade of goods for the slave traders in Africa, the shipping and sale of the slaves to the New World, and the return of produce and precious metals to England and Europe. The lure of profits overpowered the lingering moral concerns about the slave trade and slavery itself, at least for most people.

By the time Wilberforce became involved in politics, England was the world's leading slave-transporting nation, bringing great wealth to numerous merchants and shippers. There had actually been a judicial ruling in 1772 that declared

slavery inconsistent with English law. The abolitionist Granville Sharp had brought a case to Chief
Justice Mansfield, demanding that James Somerset,
a slave in Jamaica, be freed. This provided a legal
precedent for ending slavery at a later time, but it
did nothing to end the slave trade in the 1770s.

Was it a coincidence that Wilberforce came into
regular contact with the small group of abolitionists in England? Was it simply chance that at this
time Wilberforce was casting about for some worthy
purpose for his efforts in public life? Finally, was it
just fate that some who had taken up the slavery cause
were persons Wilberforce highly regarded? For those
who believe in a sovereign God at work in the lives
of believers, and who are determined to follow God's
purpose in their lives, the answer to all three questions
is an emphatic no.

Wilberforce's "conversion" to the cause of slavery
began with Captain Sir Charles Middleton, comp-
troller of the navy and head of the navy board during
and after the war with the American colonies. Middleton was also a member of Parliament and one of
the few in that body who held to Wilberforce's strong
evangelical convictions. A major influence in Middleton's spiritual development was his wife, Margaret,

who was converted early in life under the ministry of George Whitefield. She was an intellectual and also an artist and musician. More to the point, she was a person motivated to help those in need. It was said of her that she was "constantly on the stretch in seeking out opportunities of promoting in every possible way the ease, the comfort, the prosperity, the happiness temporal and eternal, of all within her reach."[14]

The Middletons' specific concern about the suffering of slaves could be traced to their vicar at Teston church, James Ramsay. Reverend Ramsay had been the surgeon on a ship commanded by Middleton in 1759. On that voyage Middleton had sent Ramsay to check on the conditions on a British ship carrying slaves, a ship the French had captured and Middleton and his crew reclaimed. Both Ramsay and Middleton were appalled at the condition of the slaves, who were suffering terribly from the plague. Subsequently, Ramsay had been rector and medical supervisor of plantations for the British colony of St. Kitts. He had seen the human suffering resulting from the slave trade and some of the evils of slavery itself. He served on St. Kitts for nineteen years, earning the disfavor of the plantation owners for his efforts to improve conditions for the slaves.

After moving to Teston, Ramsay reported to the Middletons what he had seen among slaves in the Caribbean. With their encouragement he published his "Essay on the Treatment and Conversion of Slaves in the British Sugar Colonies." His point about conversion was that the slaves would be unlikely to accept the gospel of Christ when nothing about their environment evidenced God's love at work among the whites. In response to a friendly reviewer who thought he had condoned the slave trade while condemning slavery, Ramsay wrote a second pamphlet about the "barbarous cruelty" and oppression of the slave trade itself.[15]

Moved by Ramsay's reports, the number of Teston parish members concerned about slavery began to multiply. The Middletons invited Bishop Beilby Porteus of Chester (later Bishop of London) to come to Teston to join in the discussions about slavery. Even more significant, Vicar Ramsay invited a young clergyman, Thomas Clarkson, to spend some time at Teston to join in the dialogue. Ramsay had read Clarkson's pamphlet, *Essay on the Slavery and Commerce of the Human Species*, which had won Clarkson a prize at Cambridge.

The Middletons and Ramsays were moved by the

story Clarkson told one evening at dinner about traveling to London after completing the pamphlet:

> *I stopped my horse occasionally, and dismounted and walked. I frequently tried to persuade myself in these intervals that the contents of my essay could not be true. The more, however, I reflected upon them or rather upon the authorities on which they were founded, the more I gave them credit. Coming in sight of Wade's Mill in Hertfordshire, I sat down disconsolate on the turf by the roadside and held my horse. Here a thought came into my mind—that, if the contents of the essay were true, it was time some persons should see these calamities to their end.*[16]

Clarkson's hosts at Teston could not have been more impressed by his knowledge of the subject and his passion to move from discussion into action. "Well, young man," said Middleton, "since your pamphlet does indeed contain the truth, are you ready to step forward to be the one to devote your life to ending slavery?"

"I am, indeed," responded Clarkson. "By God's grace I will devote myself fully to this cause."[17]

The encounter between William Wilberforce

and the Teston group occurred rather circuitously. Wilberforce had met the Middletons through their son-in-law and had come to know Sir Charles when he was elected to Parliament in 1784. Upon making his acquaintance, Wilberforce became a frequent guest at the Middleton home, and that friendship established the connection between him and the group concerned about slavery.

In the autumn of 1786, there was a conversation at the Middleton home about the need for a champion of abolition in Parliament. An obvious first choice was Middleton. "Sir Charles," said his wife, addressing her husband formally, as she usually did, "you ought to bring the subject before the House and demand a parliamentary inquiry in the nature of that hideous traffic. I find it so disgraceful to the British character."

Middleton agreed that someone needed to bring the situation to Parliament's attention but disagreed that he should be the one to do it. He went on to explain his limitations. He had expertise with naval issues but did not have sufficient standing in Parliament to provide leadership on the slavery issue in general. He was not a great speaker, and he did not have a close relationship with William Pitt, the prime minister.

"William Wilberforce is the one," said Middleton. "He comes from a much stronger district, and he's an excellent speaker. He's very close to Pitt. He has committed his life to Christ and would understand that this is an issue directly related to his Christian values. And unless I'm mistaken, I think he's casting about for just such a cause to which he could devote his political career."

Middleton was right about Wilberforce's readiness for such a cause. Middleton wrote to Wilberforce, asking him to bring this matter to the Parliament. Wilberforce replied that he agreed the issue was of great importance, but he felt unequal to provide leadership to the cause in Parliament. Yet in spite of his feeling of inadequacy, he accepted.[18]

Having made a tentative commitment to this endeavor, Wilberforce followed up with a series of meetings with Thomas Clarkson. Clarkson's pamphlet and subsequent research on the subject provided a body of facts and arguments on which Wilberforce could draw for the coming efforts in Parliament. The meetings in early 1787 were expanded to include others committed to the cause, including Middleton and Ramsay. Another participant was Granville Sharp, an abolition activist whose legal efforts in the Somerset case of 1772 had laid a foundation for the case against slavery.

A dinner hosted by Clarkson in March 1787 was the first semipublic occasion at which Wilberforce agreed to bring the issue to Parliament. Two other members of the Commons were present at the dinner when Wilberforce was asked to declare his willingness to become the principal sponsor of hearings and subsequent legislation. He had found one of the purposes in life he had been seeking. From that time forward, he never hesitated in giving of his energy and talent to the cause of the slaves.

The many discussions about the need to abolish slavery led to the formation in May 1787 of the Committee for the Abolition of the Slave Trade. Granville Sharp chaired the committee, and Clarkson was a member and one of its hardest workers. Most of the members were Quakers, whose behind-the-scenes work for abolition had been going on for years. They drew part of their inspiration from the efforts of the American Quaker John Woolman. Wilberforce did not formally join the abolition committee but worked closely with it in the months and years to come.

One of the major strategic discussions among Wilberforce and the other abolitionists was whether it was wise to seek the immediate end of slavery or if their first goal should be only the ending of the trade in slaves. No one involved in this effort believed that it was sufficient to end the slave trade, but after vigorous discussion the group agreed that the trade would be the first target. A factor in the decision to proceed in stages toward the ultimate goal was a constitutional issue. Supporters of slavery could have argued that Parliament had no jurisdiction over private property, especially in the colonies, which were not formally a part of England. The pragmatists in this discussion successfully argued that no one could question the right of Parliament to regulate trade, so the abolition of the slave trade was an attainable goal.

Prime Minister Pitt, the master politician, was not deeply passionate about the slave issue, though he believed that slavery should eventually be ended. He and Wilberforce discussed the prospects for abolishing the slave trade and the possibility that Wilberforce might carry the banner for this cause in the Commons. Pitt's advice to his friend came from the perspective of a political tactician, not an ideologue. Waiting too long to take this stand could deprive Wilberforce of his single greatest accomplishment in Parliament. Without such an issue, Pitt believed, Wilberforce would be forgotten a generation later.

Pitt's worries would be baseless.

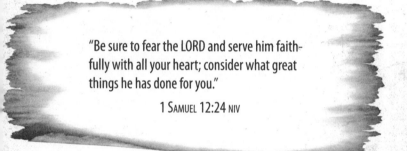

"Be sure to fear the LORD and serve him faithfully with all your heart; consider what great things he has done for you."

1 Samuel 12:24 NIV

8

TACKLING THE SLAVE TRADE

D o you think we can expect to bring this to a speedy conclusion in the Parliament? The committee and I are willing to spare no effort toward that end." Thomas Clarkson looked anxiously at his new ally. Already he trusted Wilberforce's experience and judgment in all matters relating to Parliament. The Committee for the Abolition of the Slave Trade, which Clarkson had been working with, wanted to end the slave trade as quickly as possible before tackling slavery itself.

"I would hope that we might reach our first goal of eliminating the vile trade in the next year or so, but

I have no way of knowing if that can be done," said Wilberforce. "Quite honestly, we could have a very long battle ahead of us, especially to eliminate slavery itself."

"With Parliament in recess now, what can be done before you proceed with a bill?"

Wilberforce believed Clarkson and the committee should spend every waking hour for the next few months gathering information on the evils of the trade. Thirdhand reports and speculation about what might be occurring on the high seas would get them nowhere in the House of Commons. They needed indisputable eyewitness evidence, and they needed willing and creditable people who would agree to testify. Someone had to witness the way the slaves were captured and loaded on the ships, and the kind of treatment they received while crossing the Atlantic. "We must have facts. We must have numbers. We must be able to show that the slave trade is a poor investment, since large numbers of the slaves die before they even reach the West Indies and America."

Clarkson was well qualified to do this research because of his previous study of slavery. "Set about your work as though you don't know a thing," Wilberforce urged. "Leave no stone unturned. I'll see that you are given access to the documents in the Custom House and elsewhere, but you can't limit your investigation to London. You must go to Bristol and the other ports where the ships are coming and going. You must find people willing to tell what they've seen in Africa, on the high seas, and in the colonies. With persuasion, some will be willing to testify in our hearings. Others won't, but you can use their evidence. Of course, if you do your job well, your reputation will precede you and the defenders of slavery will do all they can to hinder your work."

WILLIAM WILBERFORCE ON PERSEVERANCE

Each of us has a work to accomplish that has to do with our eternal well-being, a work to which we are naturally indisposed. We live in a world full of things that distract our attention and divert our efforts; a deadly enemy is always on hand to seduce and beguile us. If we persevere, then success is certain, but we must never stop trying. We are called to a life of continual resolution, self-denial, and activity.

Clarkson first went to Bristol to begin gathering information, going about his work with all the diligence that Wilberforce and the abolition committee had hoped for and expected. Some of those he met were willing to cooperate fully, such as the retired surgeon Alexander Falconbridge, who had served on four slaving ships. Others were cautious about talking to him for fear word would get to their former or future employers in the trade.

When Clarkson doubted the accuracy of some statements he received, he traced the reports to their sources. For example, he measured a particular ship to confirm that it was designed to give each slave only three square feet of deck space. When he began to discover that the crew members of many slave ships were treated much worse than those on other ships, he tracked down the records of the ships to confirm the reports of large numbers of sailors' deaths.

Clarkson went from Bristol to Gloucester, Worcester, and Chester. Fortunately, Alexander Falconbridge was willing to go with Clarkson to provide some physical protection and help convince the skeptics that the information they were gathering was accurate. Clarkson gathered physical evidence related to the mistreatment of slaves, purchasing such things as shackles, thumbscrews, and other instruments of torture. He was able to collect information from literally thousands of seamen and the cargo they carried. He returned to London with a large supply of evidence, a deep sadness about the inhumanity revealed by his sources, and a determination that there would be no turning back in the abolition movement.[19]

Wilberforce gave notice of his intentions when Commons was back in session.

> *Mr. Speaker, I rise to give notice that in the next session I will be ready to offer my bill that would bring an end to the slave trade. We have just celebrated the birth of our Savior, Jesus, and I can think of no better time than this to extend the compassion of our Lord to the suffering of hundreds of thousands of our brethren from the continent of Africa. I will not go into our case today, but suffice it to say that the weight of evidence on the side of abolishing this horrible trade is very convincing. I shall be most happy to pass along some of this evidence to my esteemed colleagues in anticipation of our debate and action in the future.*

"Mr. Speaker, I rise in support of the honorable gentleman from Yorkshire," said Charles James Fox, who had served in Parliament for twenty years.

I must confess that I had intended to take the first step in this noble cause before it was brought by my friend, Mr. Wilberforce. I do not resent for a minute that he has taken the first step. I trust and believe we will come to see the merits of this case and will end the brutality that has sullied the reputation of our empire. Please join me in welcoming this effort on behalf of England and the people of Africa.

Perhaps the goodwill of the holiday season and the favorable response he received when he announced the plans for a slave trade bill gave Wilberforce the feeling that abolition was on its way toward speedy success. He also felt confident because of the support he expected from Prime Minister Pitt, as well as the mountain of evidence gathered by Clarkson. Indeed, things looked good for the cause of abolition in February 1788. King George III directed that a Privy Council committee begin an investigation of the slave trade. Clarkson's hard work began to pay off as these hearings generated the first widespread knowledge about the brutalities of the slave trade and slavery.

But the optimism of Wilberforce and the abolitionists in early 1788 was premature. The Privy Council not only provided the public with knowledge of the abolitionists' case, but it gave the opponents of abolition a chance to develop their rebuttal. Far from being victims, the slave interests argued, the slaves were being rescued from death for their crimes or from abuse or death as prisoners of war. Witnesses asserted that they had seen the jubilation of slaves on their way to a better life in the New World.

WORLD EVENTS OF 1788

Georgia, Connecticut, Massachusetts, Maryland, South Carolina, New Hampshire, Virginia, and New York, respectively, become the fourth through eleventh U.S. states.

British poet George Gordon, Lord Byron, is born in London.

Hymn writer Charles Wesley, brother of John Wesley, dies.

The British First Fleet arrives in Port Jackson (modern-day Sydney), establishing the first European colony in Australia.

Meanwhile, some of those who had given information to Clarkson about the slave trade had decided that it would be too risky to testify. In fact, one of Clarkson's possible witnesses, who had apparently been deceptive when the two of them had met in Bristol, showed up to testify for the defenders of the slave trade.

Wilberforce had not only underestimated the strength of the opposition witnesses but also failed to assess the strength of the opposition within the government. His friend William Pitt knew that the king and the other members of the royal family, along with most of the Cabinet, were firmly on the pro–slave trade side of the battle.

Pitt was in a position to predict where the members of Parliament would take their stand on the slave trade. Sizable numbers were committed to defending the interests of the ship owners, the shipping investors, and those involved in the economy of the New World. Substantial numbers of members were deeply committed to freedom of trade and the protection of personal property. They shared the sentiments of English naval hero Admiral Lord Nelson, who said he would use all the energy he had to defend the status quo in the West Indian colonies "against the damnable doctrine of Wilberforce and his hypocritical allies."[20]

In February 1788, just as the Privy Council hearings were getting under way and Wilberforce was hard at work on the presentation he would make introducing the bill in the Commons, he became severely ill. He had never been particularly strong physically, but this illness was far more serious than anything he had experienced before. He had a high fever, chronic exhaustion, and severe digestive problems. Today doctors would have diagnosed his condition as ulcerated colitis, which is partially caused by stress, but at the time, his physicians were baffled by his condition. Had he not submitted to medical care and taken a break from his duties in Parliament, he might have died before reaching his thirtieth birthday.

Wilberforce wrote from Bath in early April 1788, where he was being treated and getting rest.

My dear friend Mr. Pitt,

You know of my great affection and respect for you and that I would never call on you for help unless it were absolutely necessary. I am beginning to feel a little better from the treatments I am receiving here, but my doctors and my family members have forbidden me from returning to London for

*this session. You know that the supporters of the
slave trade have presented a very vigorous case in
the Privy Council hearings. We can't let their voices
go unchallenged and must set things in motion for
a debate in the Commons, where we will be able to
answer the many ridiculous statements given in the
committee sessions. Before I came to Bath we talked
about the possibility that I might need to prevail on
you to introduce the motion in the House and now
I must ask you to do exactly that. I know you have
far too much to handle on other fronts, but the bill
must be brought forward and in such a way that its
chances will be as strong as possible.*

Pitt agreed to Wilberforce's request to introduce
the bill, but in hindsight this may not have been a
helpful first step for the cause. The wording of Pitt's
motion was not as strong as it might have been, and
his introductory speech not as forceful. Pitt was
attempting to avoid offending the opponents of abolition and did not make the kind of passionate speech
of which Wilberforce was capable. The fact that the
Privy Council committee had not concluded its hearings meant that most members felt they lacked sufficient information to take the matter seriously.

Meanwhile, another member of Parliament, Sir William Dolben, introduced a slave trade bill without coordinating his efforts with Wilberforce and the main abolition leaders. Dolben's bill would place a modest limit on the number of slaves that could be carried on a ship, and this limit would expire in a year. This effort fell far short of ending the slave trade and therefore might not enlist the backing of the strongest abolition voices. Passing the bill would accomplish little, and its defeat could have dire consequences for the earlier bill introduced by Pitt.

Had Wilberforce been on the scene, he most likely would have persuaded Dolben to withhold his measure until the Pitt bill was considered. The Dolben bill did pass, but it was tactically harmful to the abolition cause. It allowed members who were not sure about supporting Pitt's bill to be content with their support of the much weaker Dolben measure. It also allowed the first round of parliamentary debate to proceed without the oratorical and tactical strength Wilberforce could have provided.

Wilberforce was well enough to return to London in November, but a national political crisis delayed further progress on the abolition cause. King George III became physically and mentally ill,

WILLIAM WILBERFORCE ON PRIORITIES

When we really understand how short and uncertain our life is here, then we see things in their true proportions; we are then prompted to act out of the conviction that "the night cometh when no man can work." This thought produces a firm texture to our lives; it hardens us against the wind of fortune, and keeps us from being deeply penetrated by the cares and interests, the good or evil of this transitory state. When we have a realistic impression of the relative value of temporal and eternal things, this helps our souls maintain a dignified composure through all the vicissitudes of life. It brings our diligence to life, while it moderates our impulsive passions; it urges us to pursue justice, yet it checks any undue worry about the success of our endeavors.

and the prospects for his recovery were not good. William Pitt and the Parliament spent months trying to determine if a regent should be appointed to exercise the king's powers until he either recovered or died. The king did recover, but nothing was accomplished on the slave trade issue or much of anything else until well into the New Year.

Despite his ill health, Wilberforce continued to work behind the scenes on the slave issue. Word had come to him of a bright attorney practicing in St. Kitts, a man named James Stephen, who had seen the suffering of slaves and had considerable knowledge of maritime issues. Wilberforce hoped to attract him to the cause.

Stephen was particularly concerned that the testimony of the slave trade supporters not go unchallenged. Much of the testimony was so ridiculous that most would not give it serious thought, but some was plausible enough to require a serious rebuttal. Stephen's problem was that any open support of Wilberforce's work would be the end of his law practice in St. Kitts, and he had a large family to support.

For now, he could only serve as a source of reliable information and tactical advice. He was also willing to help Wilberforce prepare for the debates in the Commons. "Mr. Wilberforce, you are absolutely right in what you are doing. Don't give up, no matter what kind of opposition you may face in the days ahead," he counseled. James Stephen's encouragement and help would be important in the days ahead.

The release of the Privy Council report on the hearings helped provide information to the members, but there were many who wanted members to pay more attention to the testimony of slavery's defenders. Wilberforce worked with Pitt to develop a set of resolutions built on the testimony and continued to work hard to prepare himself for his first presentation of the issue in the Parliament on May 12, 1789.

Speeches on major new issues in the Parliament were often lengthy, and Wilberforce went on for more than three hours. He had earned his reputation in politics partly on the basis of his speaking skill, and he was in good form in bringing the issue to the Commons. He intentionally put more emphasis on reason than on speaking style. He traced the slave trade through its course, showing its negative impact on Africa, the loss of life and suffering on the trip across the ocean, and the capacity of the

West Indies to continue their plantation economy without new slaves being imported. He drew on the testimony before the Privy Council, using part of it as evidence and rebutting the testimony of supporters of the trade. He had prepared for the speech for weeks, but he had only a few notes in front of him. Edmund Burke compared his clarity and force with the legendary orator Demosthenes.

If careful preparation and excellent speaking guaranteed success, the fight against the slave trade would have been a short one, but the debate on the issue continued for days until the defenders of the slave trade succeeded in arguing that the House must constitute itself a committee of the whole to take further evidence and testimony. This tactic was successful in blocking action for the moment.

As the session ended, Wilberforce pled with his colleagues to act. "We can no longer plead ignorance," he said, "we cannot turn aside." But that is exactly what the Commons did when it adjourned in late June. There was to be no quick solution to the slave trade question.

Learn to do right! Seek justice, encourage the oppressed. Defend the cause of the fatherless, plead the case of the widow. "Come now, let us reason together," says the LORD. "Though your sins are like scarlet, they shall be as white as snow; though they are red as crimson, they shall be like wool.

ISAIAH 1:17–18 NIV

9

THE REFORMATION OF MANNERS

Wilberforce's work on abolition has been much acclaimed, but from the very beginning of his work on the slave trade, he felt equally called to bring about the reform of many other evils in society. An October 25, 1787, entry in his journal emphasizes the broad calling that he felt God was giving him at that time. He wrote, "God Almighty has set before me two great objects: the suppression of the slave trade and the reformation of manners."[21]

Indeed, Wilberforce saw moral reform and abolition as two distinct callings. At the time, he thought both causes could be taken on at the same time and both could succeed in relatively short order. Forty years later, slavery was still legal. The work on moral reform, however, was actually somewhat successful rather quickly. One notable difference was that the battle against slavery took place in the public's view and efforts for moral reformation occurred in less obvious ways.

Those who didn't realize how profound Wilberforce's change of values had been in the course of about two years might have been surprised when they first heard about his work on moral reform. He seemed to be questioning the entire way of life of the wealthy, a way of life he had experienced for years. But that was exactly his point: He had experienced this way of life from childhood through early adulthood until his commitment to Christ. He was now ready to call his countrymen to a higher moral standard.

For the wealthy in the eighteenth century, there were few moral constraints. Gluttony and drunkenness were part of the life of conspicuous consumption. Heavy gambling was another measure of one's wealth. The only constraint on gambling was the expectation that a person pay off his losses in due time. The nobleman could be sarcastic and rude to his peers, especially to the lower classes, but must be ready to defend his own honor when insulted, usually by fighting a duel. The noblewoman must produce a male heir, but the husband and wife were both free to be unfaithful to each other, as long as children were produced and properly raised by their domestic staff.

The poor, of course, were excluded from most of the vices of the wealthy, except for the many glimpses they were given when working as domestic servants. Child labor was common in the early stages of industrialization, causing some to question the efforts to eliminate slavery when working conditions for the poor at home were so horrible. The poor could not afford the kind of liquor favored by the rich but had plenty of opportunities to consume their meager resources on cheap liquor. They couldn't afford to gamble or dine and drink at the expensive clubs, but they had their own diversions, including bullbaiting, cockfighting, and the public execution of criminals. The poor probably were no better or worse than the wealthy in their sexual conduct, in terms of biblical standards.[22]

While abolition had a clear solution—the passage of legislation to outlaw first the slave trade and then slavery itself—the moral conditions that agitated Wilberforce at the time had no easy remedy. Legislation was not the answer. The evangelical revival movement, which was aimed toward a complete change of life, away from the vices of the wealthy and the poor, did not reach the privileged classes, which remained untouched by the messages and calls to repentance of evangelical preachers like John Wesley and George Whitefield.

In the campaign for moral reform, Wilberforce decided to work behind the scenes, quietly gathering political support and leaving others in charge of the actual campaign.

The first step toward national moral reform, the reissuing of a previous royal proclamation on morals, happened quickly and easily. Wilberforce enlisted the help of his friend and political ally William Pitt, and it was he who persuaded the Archbishop of Canterbury, John Moore, to carry the request to the royal family. With the support of Queen Charlotte, the Archbishop talked with King George III, who readily agreed to reissue the proclamation and did so on June 1, 1787. Because Wilberforce first wanted to be sure about the support of national leaders, he insisted that the issuing of the proclamation be done without public notice.

The proclamation's stated purpose was "the Encouragement of Piety and Virtue; and for the preventing of Vice, Profaneness and Immorality." Much of the text was carried over from previous sovereigns and from George's first proclamation. Some of its statements were general, calling on the king's subjects to help reform "persons of dissolute and debauched lives." Other statements were specific, such as the prohibition of gambling on Sunday and mandatory attendance at church. The evils Wilberforce despised were all forbidden in the proclamation—prostitution, excessive gambling, drunkenness, and pornography.

King George added a preamble to the proclamation calling particular attention to the problems of the day:

> Whereas we cannot but observe with inexpressible concern, the rapid progress of impiety and licentiousness, and that deluge of profaneness, immorality, and every kind of vice, which to the scandal of our holy religion, and to the evil example of our loving subjects, have broken in upon this nation: We, therefore, have thought fit, by the advice of our Privy Council, to issue this our Royal Proclamation, and do hereby declare our Royal purpose and resolution to discountenance and punish all manner of vice, profaneness and immorality, in

WILLIAM WILBERFORCE ON STANDARDS

Above all, let us guard against the temptation, to which we are all susceptible, of lowering our standards to match our lives, rather than raising our lives to match our standards. Let's be honest with ourselves and find out the worst about ourselves; when we do, we should allow the knowledge to move us emotionally. We shouldn't try to immediately smother the pain we feel with a sense of false peace, but instead we should patiently carry around with us a deep conviction of our ineptitude and failure, a realistic sense of our weakness and many infirmities. This cannot be an unhealthy state of mind for those who are commanded to "work out their salvation with fear and trembling."

all persons, of whatsoever degree or quality,
within this our Realm, and particularly in such
as are employed near our Royal Persons. . . .[23]

If words alone could produce reform, Wilberforce could have taken great comfort in a completed project. He knew, though, that the statement by itself would mean little. The proclamation did contain some tools for enforcement, directing ministers to read the statement at least four times a year after worship. It also directed the sheriffs in each county to enforce the proclamation. But of much greater importance was Wilberforce's continued work behind the scenes to carry out a "top down, bottom up" plan.

Wilberforce recruited a number of persons of high social standing to form a "Proclamation Society" to give visibility to the work of moral reform. For this group he recruited two kinds of persons. The first were people of high social standing who were not known as spiritual leaders or even as great moral role models. Wilberforce asked the Duke of Montagu, the Master of the Horse, to be president of the Proclamation Society; the duke's brother, the Earl of Ailesbury, to be another member; and the Duke of Manchester to join, as well. Wilberforce was conscious that many of his peers thought he had gone overboard with his new evangelical experience and wanted the moral reform movement to have broad social and political support. But other key leaders of the group were Wilberforce's evangelical allies from the abolition movement, Sir Charles Middleton, Edward Eliot, Hannah More, and Henry Thornton.

Wilberforce expanded the "top down" part of the movement to the grassroots level by going from one national leader to another, asking for their support and calling on them to encourage the formation of local efforts in their areas to promote the proclamation. From the small core group, the list of Proclamation Society members grew to include numerous bishops and archbishops (most of whom were more significant for their social than for their spiritual leadership) and a large group of nobles. The "trickle down" approach actually worked reasonably well. Local constables, parish officers, and church wardens began calling meetings to discuss ways of using the proclamation to generate moral reform.

Previously, the burden of prosecuting criminals fell on the victims, but the reform movement began calling attention to the "victimless" crimes, including the examples mentioned in the proclamation—drunkenness, prostitution, and gambling. People came to accept Wilberforce's reasoning that violent crimes, which resulted in endless numbers of public hangings, had their seed in the proliferation of lesser crimes in each community.

Supplementing these organizational efforts, some excellent writers began to call on people at both the top and the bottom levels of society to reform their lives. Hannah More, one of the first members of the Proclamation Society, was a talented playwright and poet and a member of the Blue Stocking literary group in London. She had experienced a conversion experience similar to Wilberforce's and began writing material on spiritual and moral issues. Among her books calling for the reform of the upper classes was *An Enquiry into the Duties of Men in the Upper and Middle Classes of Society*. Hannah More called on members of her own class to become examples of moral living. She also began writing inexpensive tracts directed to the lower classes. She entitled one of her series of tracts *Village Politics*, featuring a character named "Will Chip." Millions of copies of the tracts were sold and read.[24]

WILLIAM WILBERFORCE ON HOLINESS

The true Christian desires holiness—but what is the nature of true holiness? It is nothing else than the restoration of God's image to humanity. This is something we never acquire with our own strength; all our hopes of possessing it rest totally on the Divine promises of the Holy Spirit's power in our lives. First, however, we must open our hearts to the gospel of Christ. In other words, our holiness cannot precede our reconciliation with God. Our holiness is not the cause of our salvation, but its effect.

Did Wilberforce's work on moral reform work? There were some indications of improvement in the national morality. A number of highly placed people resigned their memberships in the clubs, began having regular times of family prayer, and observed the Lord's Day appropriately. People began taking their faith more seriously, and the quality of the clergy began to improve. The number of clergy who held their positions simply for the income, with no thought of providing spiritual leadership, declined. Previously one would have had to look far and wide in the Church of England to find spiritual strength among its ministers.

Wilberforce left the reform effort's success for God to judge. He saw much evidence of great improvement in the country, for which he took no credit. His goal had been to work quietly but persistently on these tasks, with no one receiving credit or blaming him for what had been done. "My little part for spiritual renewal in England has been quiet, but it may be the greatest legacy of my life," he concluded.

While he deserved considerable credit for the nation's renewal, Wilberforce praised many others for sustaining him through this endeavor and many others. One place—Clapham—became the wind beneath his wings.

> Blessed is the nation whose God is the Lord,
> the people he chose for his inheritance.
>
> PSALM 33:12 NIV

10

BATTERSEA RISE

B attersea Rise, William, that's the answer."
      Puzzled, Wilberforce looked at his friend
Henry Thornton.

"You know it's much larger than my family and I
need. I'd like you to move here, and I'd like us to think
about others who could join us. That way, we could
pray together, enjoy fellowship with one another, and
work on important projects for the advancement of
the kingdom of God. You know the pressures of public life. This—Battersea Rise—can be a retreat where
we plan our spiritual battles."

Wilberforce rubbed his chin and thought for a
moment. "I agree that the location would be good
for me, especially while Parliament is in session.

I could be away from the chaos of Westminster but not so far as to make travel impossible. And. . .I like the name, too."

Thornton and a cluster of evangelical Christian leaders, including Edward Eliot and Charles Grant, who met at Battersea Rise in a town called Clapham would come to be crucial in what Wilberforce became and in what he accomplished. The Clapham group had its roots in a group of evangelicals in Parliament who were sometimes called the "Saints," a name not always intended as a compliment.

The mentoring and encouragement Wilberforce received at Battersea Rise were a continuation of the help he received during the initial months of struggle when he was finding himself spiritually. John Newton, who helped Wilberforce understand that he could serve Christ by continuing his career in politics, continued as an encourager for many years. Newton testified during the Privy Council hearings, drawing on his direct knowledge of the slave trade. Newton and Wilberforce saw each other regularly, and there were times when Newton listened sympathetically to Wilberforce's expressions of discouragement and urged him to persist in the work. One of the ways Newton helped Wilberforce was by introducing him to a number of significant persons who also became spiritual mentors to Wilberforce, including Henry Thornton and Hannah More.

One of Wilberforce's spiritual heroes and role models from an earlier generation was John Wesley, whose ministry and work had done so much to call the people of England back to a meaningful faith in Christ. Just before Wesley died, he wrote to Wilberforce, urging him not to give up his efforts to bring an end to the "execrable villainy [slavery], which is the scandal of religion, of England, and of human nature." He went on, in what must have been one of the most treasured messages Wilberforce ever received:

> *Unless God has raised you up for this very thing, you will be worn out by the opposition of men and devils, but if God be for you who can be against you? Are all of them together stronger than God? Oh, be not weary of well-doing. Go on in the name of God, and in the power of His might, till even American slavery, the vilest that ever saw the sun, shall vanish away before it. That He that has guided you from your youth up may continue to strengthen in this and all things, is the prayer of, dear sir, your affectionate servant, John Wesley.*[25]

WILLIAM WILBERFORCE ON GRATITUDE TO GOD

Our hearts become tender when we contemplate this unique act of love and kindness. We grow desirous of imitating what we cannot help but admire. A deeper and more active love springs up inside us, and we are eager to go out and walk in the steps of our blessed Master. We want to show Him our gratitude for His goodness by bearing each other's burdens and doing all that we can to give ourselves unselfishly to each other.

To another of Wilberforce's close friends and spiritual mentors, Hannah More, belongs some credit for helping him find a balance between spiritual intensity and human warmth. Having for years lived a life of "gaiety," as it was called at the time, after committing his life to Christ, Wilberforce was at first inclined to overreact and become unduly serious. Hannah More had become equally strong in her faith, but she understood the validity of maintaining her friendships and social involvements. "I declare, I think you are serving God by making yourself agreeable. . .to worldly but well-disposed people, who would never be attracted to religion by grave and severe divines," said More to Wilberforce. She helped him understand that he could be a joyful person without compromising his Christian convictions. Hannah never married and continued for many years as a spiritual sister to Wilberforce.[26]

The idea of Battersea Rise began to take shape as Henry Thornton continued to discuss with Wilberforce who might be invited to come and live at the estate or to spend time there on a regular basis. It was agreed that Henry's brothers Samuel and Robert would be there, as would William Smith and Granville Sharp, all people with whom Henry and William had worked closely on the abolition effort. By arranging for these and other key people to live in close proximity, Thornton and Wilberforce hoped they could increase their chances of moving ahead on the slave trade effort and other causes. Battersea Rise was bound to become something of a political strategy center, considering the number of residents who were directly involved in the government, but Thornton's dream was that it become primarily a place where the residents could encourage one another spiritually and be helpful to one another when feeling discouraged.

Wilberforce accepted Thornton's invitation to take up residence at Battersea Rise. He lived in the main house for five years, moving to Broomfield Lodge on the estate when he was married. Wilberforce and the group at Clapham attracted others who were interested in the causes of abolition, moral reform, and numerous other projects, such as the Sierra Leone colony. Later the community came to be called the "Clapham Sect," but this was not an accurate label. It was in no sense a sect, with distinctive or unorthodox beliefs and practices. These were evangelicals who for the most part remained in the Church of England, determined to be a positive spiritual force in the church. They were drawn together by the opportunity for spiritual nourishment, fellowship, intellectual exchange, and political strategizing.

While the Clapham community was meant to function like a spiritual retreat center, it was anything but a place of serenity. Its residents and visitors felt free to seek each other out regularly on issues of mutual interest, which meant they engaged in conversations that went on for hours. In particular, the inner circle of the community that included Wilberforce consulted one another constantly on matters that affected the community itself and their individual lives. Wilberforce called these discussions "Cabinet Councils," giving them a more official sound than was intended. Thornton began adding to the main lodge at Battersea Rise to accommodate the growing numbers of residents and visitors, until it eventually had more than thirty bedrooms. The library became the focal point of many gatherings of Clapham people.

WILLIAM WILBERFORCE ON SPIRITUAL FRUIT

The fruits of holiness are the effects, not the cause of our being justified and reconciled with God, but that has never occurred to some people. Nor have they ever realized that, in short, this reconciliation opens wide the door of mercy, allowing the greatest and ugliest of penitent sinners to come freely inside. They do not know that if they obeyed the blessed inspiration of God's grace (that which woke them from death's sleep and moved them to seek pardon), they might simply enter. Through the life-giving influence of the Holy Spirit, they would be enabled to produce the fruits of righteousness.

Henry Thornton was successful in attracting John Venn as the rector for Clapham parish, and Venn became an important part of the attraction of living there. Wilberforce described Venn's ministry as follows: "I like him very much, and if I am not greatly mistaken, you will grow inordinately fond of him." Venn felt the same high regard for Wilberforce, describing him as "no common Christian: His knowledge of divine things and his experience of the power of the gospel are very extraordinary."[27]

Wilberforce is best remembered for his work on slavery and moral reform, but he was active in many causes that came from the collective work with the others at Clapham. The group organized numerous efforts on behalf of suffering people, including the victims of the Napoleonic wars, victims of war in Greece, North American Indians, Haitians, and others. A number of major outreach efforts of the Church of England were birthed at Clapham, including the Church Missionary Society and the British and Foreign Bible Society. Clapham residents gave considerable energy to sustain the Sierra Leone colony and worked hard to improve conditions in the British colony of India. These efforts were made possible by the willingness of Clapham residents to give of their own resources as well as their time to these causes. Henry Thornton is said to have contributed five-sixths of his considerable income to these and other causes, and Wilberforce was also generous in his support of these causes.

The deep intellectual and spiritual interaction among those at Clapham might suggest that it was a somber, joyless place. This was certainly not the case for William Wilberforce. He had taken Hannah More's advice and restored a spirit of joy and exuberance into his life after a period of spiritual introspection and struggle. Before he was married and had children, Wilberforce loved to play with the children of the Clapham community. Henry Thornton's oldest child, Marianne, recalled William's playfulness:

> He was as restless and volatile as a child himself, and during the long and grave discussions that went on between him and my father and others, he was most thankful to refresh himself by throwing a ball or a bunch of flowers at me, or opening the glass door and going off with one for a race on the lawn "to warm his feet."[28]

Being a part of the Clapham community benefited William Wilberforce in a number of ways. Before he had his own family, the community served as his family. The people of the Clapham community provided an invaluable source of help for Wilberforce's major life projects, while also providing camaraderie and friendship that took the place of socializing in the elite clubs, once Wilberforce's main social activity. When so little success was being achieved in the abolition effort for so many years, Wilberforce could count on receiving encouragement and new ideas from community members. When his health was marginal, there were people nearby to give advice and offer prayer on his behalf. In short, Clapham was the single most important factor in Wilberforce's intellectual contentment, political accomplishments, and spiritual nourishment.

"For where two or three come together in my name, there am I with them."

MATTHEW 18:20 NIV

11

RESPECT FOR ALL

If Wilberforce had only been able to interact meaningfully with fellow Christians, the impact of his life's work undoubtedly would have been limited. Surrounded as he was by a group of amiable and gifted persons at the Clapham community, he might have chosen to give his entire attention to these like-minded persons. Instead, Wilberforce made a conscious decision to interact with nonbelievers throughout his life, and these relationships were essential to his accomplishments.

Former U.S. Senator Mark Hatfield wrote the introduction to one of the editions of Wilberforce's book, *Real Christianity*. In the introduction, Senator Hatfield said it was striking to discover Wilberforce's book and see that he had, without realizing it, modeled his own life and career after the great British politician.

The two statesmen, one British and one American, had much in common, including a conversion experience after they had entered a political career. One of the things that struck Hatfield about Wilberforce was that he put great stock in dealing with others in a respectful and caring way, whether or not these persons shared his Christian values. Wilberforce "sought to continue the incarnation of the Word in loving acts of mercy, justice, and charity to those around him, even if they were adversaries."[29] Those who knew Hatfield would say the same about his interaction with colleagues during a long political career.

Both men had their closest relationships with fellow believers, but both followed the example of Christ in relating lovingly to nonbelievers. If someone had a personal need, they responded in a caring, prayerful manner. If it was a spiritual need, they sought to offer counsel and prayer. If it was a physical need, they responded with empathy. In short, they rejected the self-centeredness and arrogance that are so typically found among politicians.

Still, Wilberforce relied heavily on the counsel

and companionship of his Christian friends to keep his life on the proper course. On many occasions, he visited his friend Hannah More at the town of Bath. He remembered her advice about not becoming too intense and sober, risking turning people away from the kingdom of God, not drawing them into it. Because of her advice, he found a way to bring a measure of joyful exuberance alongside the self-discipline of the Christian life.

In their times together, William and Hannah discussed the difficulty of creating an opportunity to talk with people about what it means to be a believer. "We talk about politics and social events, we gossip about the foibles of the royal family and the rich, we talk about the weather, about the theater, but why don't we want to think about things of eternal importance?" Wilberforce wondered.

"I suppose we have to earn the right to be heard as a result of the spiritual qualities we demonstrate," Hannah replied. "When we care about those around us, they see the love of Christ through our interest. What have you been doing to turn your conversations toward spiritual things?"

Hannah's probing question made him pause. Wilberforce realized that the Holy Spirit might lead him to someone he didn't even know who was spiritually hungry. He began praying each day that he would be ready to speak to people who were seeking the Lord. He also began to keep a list of people he knew who were not believers and prayed over that list regularly, asking the Holy Spirit to open their hearts to consider their spiritual needs. "I certainly haven't given up on our friend Pitt, but I suppose there are others on the list more open to thinking about God than he seems to be."

WILLIAM WILBERFORCE ON HOPE

The Christian's hope is based not on human philosophy or strength, but on the words of Him who cannot lie, on the power of Omnipotence.

Wilberforce had decided he couldn't just wait for openings—he needed to make them. He had been experimenting with what he called "launchers," questions or comments that might steer the conversation away from trivial things to matters of eternal consequence. In a few cases, his launching comment was something like, "You and I spent considerable time together in times past, didn't we?" The response might be something like, "Yes, we did, but we're older now, and things have changed." Then he would say something like, "You're so right that things have changed, and for my part I don't regret a bit that things have changed." This gave him a chance to talk about the great change in his life that had resulted from his becoming a devoted follower of Christ. That didn't guarantee the person would want to hear Wilberforce's testimony, but at least the subject was opened.

The desire of both Hannah More and William Wilberforce to let others know what it meant to be a follower of Christ sometimes bore fruit. They and their Clapham friends had an impact on the elite in British society that went well beyond the response to the evangelical preachers of the day. But inevitably many who respected Wilberforce for his new spiritual convictions showed no desire to adopt the same way of life.

William Pitt had been one of the first to hear Wilberforce's testimony as a believer, but he closed the door on the invitation to follow him into the life of faith. Pitt remained adamant in his resistance to being evangelized. Nevertheless, the mutual respect and friendship that had drawn the two of them together early in their careers continued until Pitt's death in 1806. Wilberforce deserves much of the credit for the durability of their relationship, for they experienced a series of stressful interactions that easily could have destroyed their friendship.

Topping the list of political disagreements between William Pitt and William Wilberforce is the opposite positions they took on the continuation of the war with France in the 1790s, one of the outgrowths of the French Revolution. The issue was not whether war was an appropriate response to a challenge from one's enemies. Wilberforce was not a pacifist, but he saw much to be lost from continuing this particular war. He accurately predicted that the war would preoccupy the British government for years to come, making it virtually impossible to deal with the slave trade and parliamentary reform. Wilberforce also feared that his efforts toward the moral reform of British society would be undercut by the war with France. In reality, the brutal fate of the French aristocracy provided a warning to their counterparts in England that resisting moral reform was the wrong direction to take.[30]

Wilberforce felt sure that Pitt would be upset if he publicly opposed Pitt's stand on the war, but Wilberforce nevertheless offered an amendment in the House that called on the government to seek peace. Pitt opposed the amendment, and it was soundly defeated. Wilberforce lost sleep over the public nature of their disagreement, still believing it had been right but finding it hard to deal with the prime minister's anger. Pitt in turn was bothered by the breach in their relationship and puzzled over whether Wilberforce, whose courage and good judgment he admired, had been right on this one. After some weeks during which the political and personal rift between the two was painfully apparent to those around them, they allowed some friends to get them back together socially. They agreed to continue working together, in spite of the likelihood that Wilberforce might again be forced to put conviction ahead of friendship.[31]

A second clash between the two men was of

shorter duration. In this situation Wilberforce demonstrated that he possessed some of the same pragmatism and flexibility that typified Pitt's approach to politics. The notion of defending one's honor when opponents crossed an imaginary line between debate and insult was widely accepted in English culture at the time. In this case, Pitt accused a fellow member of Parliament, George Tierney, of intentionally undermining British foreign policy. The Speaker of the House ruled the comments inappropriate, but Pitt refused to back down.

The battle quickly escalated from a verbal confrontation into the threat of a duel. Neither of the men was willing to back off, and the duel actually occurred. Fortunately, neither was a good marksman, and perhaps neither actually intended to kill the other. By the unwritten rules of dueling, the exchange of two shots with no casualties was sufficient to end the duel and restore the honor of both men, so they were able to return to the city with the matter settled formally, if not relationally.

Wilberforce reacted swiftly to the news of the duel. He was already annoyed at Pitt for his lack of cooperation on the slave trade issue. Wilberforce was appalled at the barbarism of dueling and incensed that they would corrupt the Sabbath with such activity. Prudence would have suggested that Wilberforce talk privately with Pitt about the matter before taking action, but Wilberforce did not do this. Instead, he talked with people in London about the issue and found support for a measure to outlaw dueling. He quickly gave notice of his intent to introduce the bill. In an angry letter to Wilberforce, Pitt accused Wilberforce of introducing the anti-dueling motion as a first step toward seeking Pitt's removal as prime minister.

Wilberforce dropped his bill by the end of the week, making it clear that he had no thought of trying to bring down the Pitt government, with which he agreed most of the time. He assured Pitt that he didn't want to cause that kind of political damage. In doing so, Wilberforce couldn't resist including a statement in his letter addressing Pitt's spiritual need: "It is my sincere prayer, my dear Pitt, that you may here be the honored instrument of Providence for your country's good, and for the well-being of the civilized world; and much more that you may at length partake of a more solid and durable happiness and honor than this world can bestow."[32]

A third and final political clash between the two

men occurred not long before Pitt's death. Lord Melville, Henry Dundas, a close political ally of Pitt, had been appointed Viscount, head of the British navy. In 1805 a Committee of Navy Inquiry presented a report charging Dundas with the knowledge of or responsibility for the misuse of public funds when he had been treasurer of the navy. Opposition members of Parliament seized on the report to discredit the Pitt government, and the two sides engaged in a long verbal battle in Parliament.

Wilberforce listened carefully to the debate about Dundas, preferring to remain silent and not add fuel to the anti-Pitt vehemence. Feeling he may have been impulsive in the dueling case, Wilberforce thought long and hard about what to do in this new situation. Such debates often carried on long into the night, and this was no exception. At four in the morning, Wilberforce rose to speak. As he did, he saw the look in Pitt's eyes, a look pleading that he not lend his eloquence to the faction that wanted to impeach Dundas. Wilberforce's talk was short and to the point, expressing contempt for Dundas's unethical conduct. Prior to his speech, the expectation was that the government's position would prevail. Once Wilberforce made his speech and the vote was taken, it was a tie. The

Speaker cast the deciding vote to impeach Dundas.

Pitt was devastated by the defeat and hurt by Wilberforce's role in the outcome. Some were ready to blame Wilberforce for Pitt's subsequent physical and emotional collapse, which led to his death. But the evidence does not support this speculation. Their friendship survived the disagreement, and they were reconciled. Because they had interacted fairly and respectfully in spite of their different political approaches and spiritual values, the way remained open for them to be friends and colleagues.

Ironically, William Pitt had been a much more healthy individual than Wilberforce, but died at an early age. Wilberforce dealt with a series of ailments in his life, but by God's grace he was permitted to live much longer than Pitt.

> Do not throw away your confidence;
> it will be richly rewarded.
>
> HEBREWS 10:35 NIV

12

MATTERS OF HEALTH

Gentlemen, you've had a chance to read my report about my patient William Wilberforce," Dr. Richard Warren, one of the most prominent physicians of the day, announced to a group of his colleagues in 1788. "He hasn't even reached age thirty, but I'll be honest with you, with this many things wrong with him, I'm not optimistic that he will live another year."

"I think his chances are considerably worse than you say, sir," offered a colleague. "Barring some major change in his body or some dramatic results from treatment, I wouldn't give him more than two weeks."

Frailty seemed to run in the Wilberforce family.

Only one of his three sisters survived into adulthood. Furthermore, considering his youthful overindulgence in food and drink, it was remarkable that William's health problems were not more severe. And when Wilberforce turned from a life of indulgence to a self-disciplined lifestyle, he probably took some additional health risks. A doctor who examined him after his conversion experience warned him that fasting for spiritual purposes could have serious physical consequences for a person who was not strong. Then when Wilberforce sought to make up for his earlier study habits by spending hours reading, his doctor warned that his already poor eyesight could deteriorate even further. The doctor's prescription was one of the most common in that day: Go to Bath to partake of the mineral waters there.[33]

The waters of Bath were of some help, but Wilberforce's health continued to deteriorate in early 1788. He became ill in early January at a crucial time in his preparations for the Privy Council hearings on the slave trade, so he refused to slow down. He tried to keep going with his responsibilities during February and March, but his symptoms of high fever, terrible intestinal pain, insomnia, and weakness continued. Sometimes he went to bed to get some rest, but he was unwilling to follow the advice of his family and friends to get away from the stresses of his work in London. Instead, he took the advice of his doctors and began taking opium for his pain.

It is puzzling to the modern reader to learn of William Wilberforce's use of opium. He began taking the drug in 1788 and continued its use the rest of his life. It was the only means available for maintaining a normal life while suffering from ulcerated colitis. A variety of medications at that time contained opium, and pure opium was readily available without prescription and commonly used. Opium was even an ingredient of a syrup given to babies and a tonic used by children. No one at the time felt that Wilberforce was compromising his Christian witness by using the drug.

While little was known about the drug's effects, what was clear was that Wilberforce could never stop taking it once he had started. And considering what was known about ulcerated colitis and the available treatments, his doctors' recommendation to take opium was probably appropriate. Clearly,

Wilberforce was not taking opium for its narcotic effects and had no intention of gradually increasing the dosage. He needed relief from the pain, and his doctors advised him on the amounts he should take. Even though he had health problems for the rest of his life and continued taking opium for forty-five years, he was able to keep the dosage at an appropriate level, only increasing it temporarily when he had unusual symptoms.

Physicians today would be concerned about the effects of opium on Wilberforce's already poor eyesight. Indeed, over the course of his continued usage, his eyes became progressively worse. Certainly his long hours of intense study and the limited knowledge of corrective lenses and surgery contributed to the worsening vision, but he undoubtedly hurt his eyes from his regular opium use. He became more absentminded in later years and less diligent about his duties. Still, his life accomplishments and long service in the Parliament argue against his serious physical and emotional deterioration from the drug.

WILLIAM WILBERFORCE ON TALENT

I recommend that the great, the wise, the learned, and the successful. . .make a habit of considering their superiority, whether it is derived from nature, study, or fortune, as an undeserved gift from God. This reflection will naturally tend to create a humbler disposition, one that is more useful to God and humanity, rather than the proud self-complacency such people usually tend to feel. If they turn their hearts to God, they will find themselves filled with greater reverence, humility, and gratitude, delighting to be engaged in God's praises and work. When we realize how much we have been given, we long to be employed in the loving service of this universal Gift-Giver.

Even though Wilberforce improved considerably in March 1788 and the slave trade hearings in the Parliament were at a crucial stage, he realized how close he had come to dying. Rather than risk another relapse from the stress of continuing his work in London, he decided to take the advice of his family and doctors to get away to Bath. His willingness to disengage himself at the time and to call on Prime Minister Pitt to offer the first slave trade motion was a measure of his good sense and his confidence that others in the abolition movement would carry on the work until he could return.

Probably more important for Wilberforce's recovery than the waters of Bath and the use of opium was his willingness to set aside his worries about the abolition struggle and spend time in complete rest and solitude. He wrote about the healing effects of reading the Bible and praying "early in the fine autumn mornings when the lake used to be as calm as so much glass, and all the mountains, shrouded with vapors, compassed me round like so many sleeping lions." He wrote a prayer in his journal as he was emerging from the physical and emotional pain that had almost ruined him: "O Lord our God, thou has said unto us I will never leave you, nor forsake you. . . . Thou has supported my spirit in the days of trouble and has given me many intervals of refreshment, renewing thy loving kindness day by day."[34]

His health on the mend for the time being, Wilberforce again turned his attention to the abolition of slavery—this time, with an eye across the English Channel.

> But he said to me, "My grace is sufficient for you, for my power is made perfect in weakness." Therefore I will boast all the more gladly about my weaknesses, so that Christ's power may rest on me.
>
> 2 CORINTHIANS 12:9 NIV

13

ALLIES IN ABOLITION

Wilberforce had been thinking of going to France to see if he could generate support for the simultaneous abolition of the slave trade in France. As long as France was standing by to take over the English place in the trade, it would be difficult to get Parliament and the king to pass the slave trade measure. Not only would England lose the slave trade revenue, it would lose it to an old enemy.

Wilberforce's friend Thomas Clarkson thought Wilberforce was being horribly naive to think he could go over and make private inquiries about support for abolition in France. He was a member of Parliament, and his name was well-known. The government would soon become aware of his mission and be

WILLIAM WILBERFORCE ON SELF-DENIAL

"Mortify the flesh, with its affections and lusts," is the Christian rule, but most modern Christians practice a soft luxurious life of habitual indulgence. We seem to think that a healthy disciplined self-denial went out of style years ago along with the austerities once practiced in monasteries. Christianity calls us to a state of alert diligence and active service.

offended by his self-appointed diplomacy. The French revolutionary forces might welcome him with open arms, and that in itself would make him an enemy in the king's palace.

"You may be right, Clarkson," Wilberforce admitted, "but you're the only other one who can undertake this mission. This is absolutely crucial to our cause, no matter what happens to the French government. You've got to go, and you've got to find those who might begin to lay the groundwork for doing in France what we hope to do in England. We've got to win the day in our own government, but we can't let our opponents carry the day by playing the French card."

Thomas Clarkson agreed to go to France and was at first encouraged by the support for abolition he found among French liberals. He sent Wilberforce reports about the numerous leaders who agreed that the ideals fueling the French Revolution were directly applicable to the evils of slavery. But he soon encountered the same distrust of the British that mirrored the English dislike of the French. People in France asked Clarkson if he could assure them that the English would pass the abolition measure if the French did. Even though he believed that Parliament would ultimately pass the abolition measure, there was no way he could guarantee when it might pass and certainly no way to predict that French action would become a key factor in the English taking similar action.

When Parliament reconvened in January 1790, Wilberforce once again had to deal with the tactics of his opponents, who wanted to prolong the process by asking for more hearings. The proslavery witnesses expected to go first in the hearings and hoped to exhaust the patience of House members before the abolitionists got a fair hearing. Wilberforce proposed an alternative process, referring the matter to a special committee. Knowing antiabolition forces would argue that referring the matter to a small committee would limit their right to be heard, Wilberforce proposed that the committee open its sessions to all members who wanted to listen and speak. Some members might take this opportunity at first, but they would

WORLD EVENTS OF 1790

President George Washington gives the first State of the Union address.

The Supreme Court of the United States meets for the first time, in New York City.

American scientist and statesman Benjamin Franklin dies.

Adam Smith, Scottish economist, dies.

 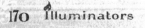

eventually lose interest. Then the committee could proceed with gathering evidence.

Wilberforce's procedural tactics were successful. He outmaneuvered those who wanted to block any further consideration of the issue and got the House to refer it to a select committee. He and fellow member William Smith chaired the hearings that continued for many months and gathered thousands of pages of material. Antiabolition witnesses had heard most of the abolition arguments and presented arguments they considered to be strong. They insisted that the slaves were mostly criminals and prisoners of war, deserving little sympathy. They asserted that there were no commercial opportunities in Africa apart from the slave trade. And they insisted that life on the slave ships was not as unpleasant as abolitionists had claimed.

Opponents of abolition did their best to wear down the committee and minimize the chances for the abolitionists to respond, continuing their testimony into April. Wilberforce had his trusted ally Thomas Clarkson at his side in the hearings, preparing responses to the points being made and sometimes going to check on facts and locate additional witnesses. When proslavery testimony ended in April, antiabolitionists tried to get the House to act on the measure immediately. Wilberforce won a second tactical victory, blocking the motion to take up the abolition measure before further testimony.

Even though Parliament adjourned before all of the abolitionist testimony could be presented, abolitionists felt they had effectively responded to the pro–slave trade forces. Moreover, the hearings generated broader interest in the question, and the public began to take note of the morality of slavery through popularly available material. Numerous pamphlets called on the people to understand the evils of the slave trade. Abolitionists circulated many copies of a detailed sketch Thomas Clarkson had prepared, showing the unbelievable crowding on the slave ships.

Many people read and were moved by William Cowper's poem "The Negro's Complaint," which contained the lines, "Is there, as ye sometimes tell us, / Is there One who reigns on high? / Has He bid you buy and sell us / Speaking from His throne, the sky?" Abolitionists circulated an edition of the poem, calling on readers to talk about it over tea. In still another medium, Josiah Wedgwood, the great ceramicist, designed a cameo depicting an African slave pleading for mercy. Its inscription was meant to generate compassion and guilt: "Am I Not a Man and a Brother?"[35]

WILLIAM WILBERFORCE ON COMPASSION

Get used to paying close attention to all those who live in a careless and inconsiderate world, who are in such imminent danger and are so ignorant of their peril. Think about these people, until you feel pity for them. This sympathy will melt your heart. Once there is room in your heart for Christ's love, this will produce— almost without your noticing—a habitual feeling of gentle sympathy.

Growing public concern about slavery was Wilberforce's main asset when Prime Minister Pitt called a national election in 1790. Wilberforce was not sure how he would fare in the election. He feared that his heavy involvement in the slave trade issue, his difficulty in returning to Yorkshire as often as he thought he should, and the overwhelming task of keeping up with his constituents' correspondence might all work against him. But he participated in the canvass, and at the end of three weeks, it was clear that he and his fellow incumbent, Henry Duncombe, had ample support to make a challenge impossible. The election came at a good time for Wilberforce, in a way, assuring him he had the backing of his constituents in order to proceed with the abolition effort.

As so often in the past, one of Wilberforce's trusted friends was there to offer more than a sounding board.

"If you'll pardon my candor, William, with your eyesight, you'll have a hard time getting through the piles of material presented to the Privy Council and then to the select committee," offered Thomas Babington. "You know, I think Thomas Gisborne would be happy to make room for us at Yoxall Lodge. What do you say? We would be free of distractions and I can read over the material more quickly than you. We can discuss it, make notes, and get ready for the next round of hearings and debates. I can set aside other projects for as long as it takes to work on this and for as many hours a day as we can productively deal with it."

Wilberforce was intrigued and beholden to his friend. "You always know what I need. A quiet place, and the help of someone like you to think through what may still be lacking in our case, seems an ideal solution. As usual, you are a wonderful gift from God!"

Had Wilberforce and Babington known that the decade of the 1790s would see one defeat after another for the abolition cause in Parliament, it might have been hard to spend so much time preparing their case. But the formidable challenges ahead called for all the effort and intellectual strength they could muster. The first of these challenges was the news of a slave uprising in Santo Domingo (later called the Dominican Republic). There were ten times as many slaves in the colony as white colonists, and there was a large group of what were then called mulattoes who took the side of the slaves in the revolt. The revolt was unsuccessful, but two thousand whites were killed, and the incident gave the proslavery faction in Parliament a chance to argue that the abolition effort was directly responsible for slave unrest. A proslavery member of Parliament claimed, without solid evidence, that the slaves acted on the assumption that Wilberforce and his allies would eventually succeed in freeing them. Even though the abolitionists' objective was simply to cut off the transport of slaves, the pro-slave voices seized on the uprising to argue that peace and economic stability in the West Indies were threatened by the debate on abolition.

Regardless of the prospects for success, Wilberforce put all his rhetorical skill and energy into the debate that began on the floor of the Commons in 1791. The proceedings began in the late afternoon on April 18 and continued with only short recesses until the early hours of April 20. Like Wilberforce's first major speech on the subject two years before, this was a long one, lasting four hours. He used the months of preparation to good advantage, restating the moral high ground he had earlier claimed and answering the points made in the hearings by the defenders of the slave trade. He spoke of new evidence of cruelty in the seizure of slaves before their transport and new reports of despicable conditions during their shipment. He argued that the West Indian planters had falsely asserted that the colonies could not survive without a steady supply of new slaves. In fact, he said, eliminating the supply would motivate the planters to treat the existing slaves more humanely, and a healthier population of slaves would assure their numbers would continue to be sufficient and diminish the likelihood that they would revolt.

Hours of debate followed Wilberforce's opening speech. Numerous defenders of slavery spoke, but strong voices presented the abolition side, including those of William Pitt, Charles James Fox, and Edmund Burke. A few members declared their intention of shifting to the abolition side of the vote. But concerns about developments in France and fears of the slave revolt in Santo Domingo turned the sentiment in the House against the abolition case. There were some sixty members with direct ties to shipping and to the West Indian colonies, and they voted as a block against Wilberforce. The result was a crushing defeat: 163 "no" votes and 88 "yea" votes.

Most politicians would have taken the defeat as reason enough to suspend the abolition efforts for a more promising time. Wilberforce was not an ordinary politician and was not about to give up. He made it clear after the 1791 defeat that he would continue pursuing the cause, no matter how little progress there was toward success. His determination gave courage to the abolition movement and gave birth to a new kind of local support network, what we would call grassroots lobbying.

The Committee for the Abolition of the Slave Trade organized local abolition associations around the country. The national committee provided information to the local groups by preparing and distributing a one-volume summary of the material presented at the slave trade hearings. Local enthusiasts began circulating petitions against the slave trade and delivering these to Parliament. This was not a common practice in that day, and even Wilberforce wondered whether this kind of popular expression to the Parliament was appropriate. Even more radical in the minds of some was the local abolitionists' organizing of sugar boycotts. As mild as this action might appear to modern observers, it certainly wasn't standard practice at the time, and it raised fears associated with the expressions of radical democracy in France.

Principled reformers sometimes find their greatest challenge among their supporters, those who profess belief in their cause but advocate a cautious and gradual approach to change. This was the fate of the abolition movement in 1792. True to his word after his defeat the year before, Wilberforce presented his abolition measure in April 1792, again accompanied by a powerful speech. He ended the speech with a statement of gratitude that even though not successful, he "had the bliss of remembering that he had demanded justice for millions who could not ask it for themselves."[36] Judging from the vote the year before, the chances of getting the bill passed were not good. Then Henry Dundas rose to speak, expressing support

for the measure but proposing to amend it by insert-
ing one word, the word *gradual* before *abolition*. The
effect of his amendment would be that English ships
would no longer be allowed to carry slaves to foreign
destinations but would be given until 1800 to continue transporting slaves to English-controlled destinations. Later the date was moved to 1796.

WORLD EVENTS OF 1792

The guillotine is first used in France.

The French monarchy is abolished and replaced by the
First Republic.

Composer Giacchino Rossini is born in Pesaro, Italy.

British poet Percy Blythe Shelley is born.

American naval captain John Paul Jones dies.

Swedish king Gustav III is assassinated.

One might commend Dundas for practicing the politics of the possible, but for Wilberforce and his strongest supporters, even a delay of four years was unacceptable. At the time they had no way of knowing that abolition would not succeed for another decade. They accepted Dundas's profession of belief in the evil of the slave trade but feared a modest delay could lead to a series of postponements.

This was the kind of struggle that often arose within reform movements between idealists and pragmatists, those who wanted change immediately and those who felt a gradual shift was sufficient. Interestingly, William Pitt, who at times was hesitant about continuing to back abolition, attacked Dundas's delaying amendment. He described the amendment as essentially a defeat of abolition. In spite of his efforts, the amendment passed and the amended motion in turn passed 230 to 85. Wilberforce and the abolitionists were disappointed, but they were relieved when the House of Lords let the measure die.[37]

The war with France that began in 1793 had a devastating affect on the abolition effort because of the fear that France would step in to operate the slave trade if and when England withdrew from it. One of the things the British could almost always agree on was their dislike for the French. Moreover, differing views about the need for war and its continuance pushed most other business off the agenda in Parliament. So desperate was Wilberforce to keep his issue alive that he actually offered Dundas's gradual measure in 1793, but even that failed to pass either the House of Commons or the House of Lords. One could almost call Wilberforce a fanatic on the slave trade issue, for he tried some form of it every year during the remainder of the 1790s, even though his prospects for success were slim. In 1793 and 1794 he tried a variation on Dundas's bill directing that slaves could not be carried to other nations but the traffic could continue to English soil. Even with this modest change, he was unsuccessful.

In 1796 and during each of the remaining years of the century, Wilberforce returned to his original effort to completely and immediately abolish the slave trade. The number of members voting on his side was small during these years, reflecting the lack of interest in the subject. The margin of defeat varied from year to year, but there was no real sign of hope. One of the most discouraging votes was in 1796 when the vote was scheduled on the evening that a new opera was opening in London. Only 144 members voted, and Wilberforce lost by four votes.

As the century ended, the prospects for abolition were not at all good. Thomas Clarkson, one of the most able workers in the movement outside Parliament, was in poor health and dropped out of the movement. Most of the other members of the Committee to Abolish the Slave Trade had become discouraged, and the committee no longer met regularly. Prime Minister Pitt had fought hard against the Dundas effort to delay abolition, but in 1797 he supported a measure that would have given the assemblies in the West Indian colonies the authority to decide about allowing slaves to be imported. This would have given Pitt a chance to appear supportive of a form of abolition but would have done nothing to reduce the trade. No one in the colonial legislatures had any intention of restricting slavery.

The battles against slavery had been discouraging, but Wilberforce clung to hope, kept his physical condition stable, and remained in relatively good spirits. Only unshakable hope grounded in his Christian convictions could have kept Wilberforce going during this decade. Only his extraordinarily intense determination could have helped him look ahead to the day when he would succeed.

If the LORD delights in a man's way, he makes his steps firm; though he stumble, he will not fall, for the LORD upholds him with his hand.

PSALM 37:23–24 NIV

14

REAL CHRISTIANITY

Hannah looked expectantly at her dear friend. Gray half-moon bags under his eyes gave away his physical condition, but clearly his mind was running vigorously. "I can tell this is not just a social visit, William," she began.

He nodded, clearing his throat. "You are a gifted writer and I certainly am not. But almost from the moment I began trying to explain to others my convictions as a serious follower of Christ, I have felt I needed to do more than just talk to people. I think I should begin to put my thoughts on paper in some form or another."

"Whom would you be addressing with this work?"

"Of course some readers would be my peers, like

William Pitt, who have listened politely to my talk about giving their lives in surrender to Christ as Savior but have never been convinced it is something they should do. I would also hope that my book might affect some people the way Philip Doddridge's book affected me."

"What encouragement have you had from your Christian friends about this project? Are the folks at Clapham supportive?"

"I've talked with Henry Thornton, John Venn, and William Farish. They didn't try to discourage me from going ahead with the work, but I didn't really get much help from them on the content," Wilberforce admitted.

"Could you tell me in a few sentences what you feel God would have you say to your readers?"

"My main message would be that many of those who call themselves Christians fall far short of living out the essence of real Christianity. As long as we allow this inadequate form of Christianity to go unchallenged, those who are spiritually needy will never come to faith in Jesus Christ. Our nation faces many challenges at home and abroad, and now is the time for us to return to a radical faith in Jesus Christ."

"William, just remember that you're a politician,

WILLIAM WILBERFORCE ON LIVING FOR CHRIST

The very tendency that we feel to hide our faith from the world's view confirms that we are more influenced by the world's opinions than we are by God's. I would hope that simply because our faith is secret, having vanished from our conversations, replaced by a pretended freedom of feeling and conduct, that it still does exist in our private hearts. I fear, though, that we are not merely putting on a false show for others; while we weren't paying attention, our faith may have quietly been smothered. By complying with the world's habits, participating in the manners of this dissipated age, we have removed every external distinction between the Christian and the nonbeliever. We seldom find anyone who is brave enough to be different for Christ, someone who "is not ashamed of Christ."

not a theologian. Don't engage in debates with philosophers and scholars. Talk from your heart to those who are spiritually hungry. Your readers must be common people. And don't get tempted to wander into discussing the political issues of the day. Those will come and go. Your spiritual message is a timeless one. Even as passionate as you are about slavery, don't use this book to beat that drum."

Guided by the wise advice of Hannah More, Wilberforce plunged ahead with his project of writing something substantial about what it means to be a real Christian. Even though there was somewhat of a lull in the abolition struggle, there was still work to be done on the cause, and he introduced numerous bills on the slave trade during the four years he was working on his writing. And there were numerous other distractions during this time. Constituents and other politicians constantly sought him out with a variety of requests. He received a large amount of correspondence and struggled without success to keep up with it. Although his neighbors at Clapham stimulated his mind and soul and brought him much enjoyment, it was a difficult place to get serious writing done. Moreover, his health continued to be marginal.

Wilberforce was able to get his manuscript done for one reason alone: He was passionate about articulating his faith in Christ. He was as committed to thoroughgoing moral and spiritual reform as he was to the abolition of slavery. He wanted people to understand that Christianity is not about religious respectability. It is first and last the transformation of one's heart and life that makes one live in a loving way. It is living a holy and righteous life and making one's conduct fit the content of his or her prayers and Bible readings on Sunday.

WILLIAM WILBERFORCE ON SCRIPTURE

Let me remind you, that there is no middle road. If you look into your Bible, and you do not make up your mind to absolutely reject its authority, then you must admit that you have no grounds for hoping to escape the punishment that the Bible predicts. Don't think that your guilt is so little that God will not bother with it. It is ludicrous to think you can trifle with God's patience, ignoring both His invitations and His threats, refusing the offer of His Spirit of grace and the precious blood of the Redeemer. Scripture warns, "How shall we escape if we neglect so great salvation?"

The publisher Thomas Cadell was intrigued when Wilberforce showed him the manuscript of his book. "Is this about slavery?" he asked hopefully.

"No, this is not about abolition or any other political issue. Take a look at the title, *A Practical View of the Prevailing Religious System of Professed Christians in the Higher and Middle Classes in This Country Contrasted with Real Christianity.* I think that pretty well expresses the contents of the piece."

"If you were a religious scholar writing about religion, we would consider it. Since you are a politician of considerable repute, we could publish almost anything you write on national policy issues. But a book on religion by a politician? This is a very long manuscript. My guess is that it would run almost five hundred pages in length. This would be an expensive book to publish. Leave it with me, Wilberforce. I will at least read it and give it some thought. But I can make no guarantees, you understand."

"I understand. I'm not asking you to lose money on the book, but give it a careful look. These are hard times in our nation. I think there are many people who are looking for a spiritual anchor in turbulent times."

WILLIAM WILBERFORCE ON TRUE CHRISTIANITY

True practical Christianity, never forget, consists in devoting our hearts and lives to God. Real Christianity demands that we always be governed by the desire to know and do His will. Our greatest inspiration in life should be to "live to His glory." If we lack these essential prerequisites, then it matters little how likable we are, how creditable and respectable. If we lack the essence of Christianity, then we should not be complimented by being given its name.

The first part of Wilberforce's book seems to have a negative tone, for Wilberforce sets about to identify and dismiss widespread views he deems to be inadequate—views of the character of Christianity itself, of human nature, and of the nature of God. A sample of his criticism of nominal Christians is this statement early in the book:

> With Christianity, professing Christians are little
> acquainted. Their views of Christianity have been
> so cursory and superficial that they have little

more than perceived those exterior circumstances that distinguish it from other forms of religion. These circumstances are some few facts, and perhaps some leading doctrines and principles, of which they cannot be wholly ignorant. But of the consequences, relations, and practical uses of these principles, they have few ideas—or none at all.[38]

Amid his attacks on lukewarm Christians, there is a warm, positive tone to some of the passages.

If we look to the most eminent of the Scripture characters, we find them warm, zealous, and affectionate. When engaged in their favorite work of celebrating the goodness of their Supreme Benefactor, their souls appear to burn within them, and their hearts kindle into rapture. The powers of language are inadequate to express their transports of delight. They call on all nature to swell the chorus, and to unite with them in hallelujahs of gratitude, joy and praise.[39]

There are also passages that point the way to an immediate and compelling relationship with God, such as the following:

*Let us have daily intercourse with Him in prayer
and praise, seeking dependence and confidence in
dangers, and hope and joy in our brighter hours.
Let us endeavor to keep Him constantly in our
minds, and to render all our thought of Him more
distinct, lively, and intelligent. . . . The name of
Jesus is not to be to us like Allah of the Moham-
medans; or like a talisman or an amulet, worn on
the arm as an external badge and symbol of a profession, thought to preserve one from evil by some
mysterious and unintelligible potency. Instead,
we should allow the name of Jesus to be engraved
deeply on the heart, written there by the finger
of God Himself in everlasting characters. It is
our sure and undoubted title to present peace and
future glory. The assurance which this title conveys
of a bright turning toward heaven will lighten
the burdens and alleviate the sorrows of life.*[40]

Even though Wilberforce told his publisher this
was not a book about politics, he ended it with a call
to national revival, reform, and prayer:

*Boldly I must confess that I believe the national
difficulties we face result from the decline of*

*religion and morality among us. I must confess
equally boldly that my own solid hopes for the well-
being of my country depend, not so much on her
navies and armies, nor on the wisdom of her rulers,
nor on the sprit of her people, as on the persuasion
that she still contains many who love and obey the
Gospel of Christ. I believe that their prayers may
yet prevail. . . . May there be here at least a sanctu-
ary, a land of true faith and piety, where we may
still enjoy the blessings of Christianity. May there
be here in this nation a place where the name of
Christ is still honored and men may see the blessings of faith in Jesus. May the means of religious
education and consolation once again be extended to
surrounding countries and to the world at large.*[41]

In spite of the publisher's initial pessimism, he
agreed to publish a modest number of copies, never
imagining that the book would be as successful as it
was. Few today would argue that it has the literary
quality and spiritual depth of a book like C. S. Lewis's
Mere Christianity, but Wilberforce's book nonetheless
became what we today call a "best-seller." Within the
first few days, the first printing was gone, and in a few
months seventy-five hundred copies had been sold.

During Wilberforce's lifetime the book went through fifteen editions in England and twenty-five in the United States. Translations were published in French, Italian, Spanish, Dutch, and German.

At a time when success in the abolition effort was elusive, the warm praise of friends and strangers alike was a great encouragement to Wilberforce. Sir John Pennington Muncaster wrote, "As a friend I thank you for it; as a man I doubly thank you; but as a member of the Christian world, I render you all gratitude and acknowledgment. I thought I knew you well, but I know you better now, my dearest excellent Wilber."

John Newton wrote, "I have devoured it. I think you know by this time that I do not much deal in Ceremonials and compliments—but I should stifle the feeling of my heart were I wholly to suppress mentioning the satisfaction, the pleasure, the joy, your publication has given me."

Edmund Burke's doctor reported that his patient spent much of the last two days of his life reading the book and found great comfort in it.[42]

Another prominent figure, Arthur Young, known for his innovative approaches to agriculture, wrote to Wilberforce that he had purchased the book in a time of distress over the suffering and death of his young daughter. He said that he read it over and over and that "It made so much impression on me that I scarcely knew how to lay it aside." He said it had drawn him to repentance and into a new relationship with the "Great Physician of soul."[43]

A somewhat exaggerated report about the book stated, "It was read at the same moment, by all the leading persons in the nation. An electric shock could not be felt more vividly and instantaneously. Everyone talked about it. . . . It was acknowledged that such an important book had not appeared for a century."[44] Even discounting the hyperbole in the statement, Wilberforce had much to be thankful for in having found time to write the book, in being faithful to the message he felt God had given him, and in expressing the message with the same passion that energized his political efforts.

People had indeed raved about his spiritual passion. . .but so far passion of a romantic nature had eluded him. Where was the woman who could be Wilberforce's equal both intellectually and spiritually, and was there any hope that he would find her?

But may all who seek you rejoice and be glad in you; may those who love your salvation always say, "Let God be exalted!"

PSALM 70:4 NIV

15

MARRIAGE

After Henry Thornton married, Wilberforce could clearly see how happy his friend was in his new life as a husband. Wilberforce himself had been too busy to think much about marrying, or so he told himself. There was also the issue of his health, which had been so poor that he did not think marriage would be fair to any woman. Who would want to become a nurse rather than a wife? When he mentioned these thoughts to Thomas Babington, he got more than he bargained for.

"Thornton talks about little else than his hope that I will get married. There's no doubt that he and Marianne are very happy, but just because they found each other doesn't mean I would find someone."

"What kind of person might win your heart, William?"

"How can I know if I've never met such a person? But of course I haven't really been looking. I'm not interested in someone whose only goal is to bring honor to herself and her family by being linked with someone who is prominent in public life. Likewise, I don't want to consider someone who mainly wants to better herself financially. The one thing I would put above these concerns would be that this person be a good fit spiritually. Nothing would make me happier than to find someone who was as serious as I try to be in following God day by day."

Babington immediately thought of Barbara Spooner, the oldest daughter of Isaac and Barbara Spooner. She was a bit younger than Wilberforce— she was about to turn twenty-one—but an interesting and serious young woman.

Exactly two days after Babington and Wilberforce talked about the subject, William received a letter from Barbara Spooner. She said nothing about having heard about him from Babington, but the timing would suggest that he had something to do with her letter. Rather than expressing any interest in meeting him or asking about his political projects, she asked for spiritual advice. This confirmed what Babington had said about her being intent on knowing and following God's will, and it made a deep impression on Wilberforce.

Babington also may have been responsible for arranging for the two to meet each other at a dinner party the very night Wilberforce got the letter. William's entry in his diary after their meeting was appropriately understated: "Pleased with Miss Spooner."[45]

WILLIAM WILBERFORCE ON THE GRACE OF GOD

You do not need to despair. Jesus offers the gospel to people who are just like you, in the very condition where you find yourself. The gospel's promises are for those who are "weary and heavy-laden" under the burden of their sins, to those who thirst for the water of life, to those who feel themselves "tied and bound by the chain of their sins," who abhor their captivity and long for deliverance. Be happy! The grace of God has visited you and "has brought you out of darkness into his marvellous light," "from the power of Satan unto God."

At church the next day, on Easter Sunday, he gave up on fully concentrating on worshiping the risen Savior. He confided in his diary at the end of the day that he mingled his adoration of God with his complete infatuation with Barbara Spooner. In literally a day's time, he had gone from being intrigued with this person he had not yet met to fantasizing about being married to her.

The expression "whirlwind courtship" hardly does justice to the pace of the romance between William and Barbara during the week after they first met.

William was thirty-eight, nearly twice Barbara's age, but he pursued her like a boy just out of puberty. Zachary Macaulay served as their escort for their first official date, and from that point the two were together almost every day for the rest of the week. They dined at the Pump Room and at the Spooners' house. By Saturday, exactly a week after they first met, Wilberforce was saying in his journal that he was totally in love. Then he told Babington this in person.

"It's only been a few days since we talked about the idea of me meeting someone, and all of a sudden, here she is! You were absolutely right that she fits all the things that are important to me in a life companion. This has been an utterly amazing week since we met."

"I don't have any reason to think that you aren't right for each other," said Babington slowly. "But shouldn't you give yourself more time and allow God to show you more clearly whether this is right for you? There's so much at stake for both of your futures."

"There's something I haven't told you," Wilberforce admitted. "I already wrote to her, asking for her hand in marriage. The letter is on its way."

"You have completely taken leave of your senses!

WILLIAM WILBERFORCE ON PLEASING GOD

If we really want to please God, we will always seek the path that He wants for us. We will not wait lazily, satisfied that we have not refused any opportunity to do good that was forced upon us. Instead, we will pray to God for wisdom and spiritual understanding, so that we may have the insight to discern opportunities for serving Him in our world. We will be judicious in finding ways to do good, and wise as we carry out these opportunities.

Please, for your sake and mine, as well as Barbara's, go find the letter and hang on to it for at least a few days."

"I think you're wrong about my being too hasty, Thomas. Still, I value your judgment and will see if I can intercept the letter. But if not, be assured that I know her to be a great and godly woman, the answer to all my prayers. Waiting for years would not reveal her to be anything other than a wonderful gift of God to me."

William's proposal letter had gone on its way before he could intercept it, and Barbara replied quickly and affirmatively. They had no intention of having a long engagement, but William had to deal with some urgent government business, including clearing himself of some false charges that he had been partly responsible for a mutiny of some sailors. By the end of May, William was able to return to see Barbara, and they were married in a quiet ceremony at the parish church of Walcot in Bath. William's friends set aside their misgivings about the hastiness of the courtship and extended their congratulations and best wishes.

Inevitably, some thought that William could have chosen someone better suited to him and his career. They noted that Barbara was much less outgoing than William, but Wilberforce liked the fact that she was not attracted to the social opportunities open to those prominent in national life. He was much more interested in spending time with those close to him than cultivating political and social acquaintances. He had been very close to a number of friends, and now he looked forward to even closer relationships with his own family.

Barbara found it hard to adjust to the endless parade of guests and visitors to their house. He loved seeing people but realized that for her sake and for his own health, he needed to cut back on some of the intrusion of political visitors to their home. Barbara's concern about his involvement with others was something he understood and accepted. She had little interest in becoming a great hostess, but he was not particularly concerned about impressing others, either. He assumed his friends could accept her for who she was, and his deep love for her allowed him to overlook her faults.

In spite of his busy political life, William shared Barbara's desire for a large family, and they began immediately, having their first two children, William and Barbara, in the first two years after their wedding. God blessed them with three more sons and another daughter. They lived for eleven years in a house at Clapham they bought from Edward Eliot's estate and were able to continue to benefit from the close friendships of that community and the access to political and spiritual counsel. The community valued children, and William enjoyed the time he could spend with his own children there, just as he had enjoyed playing with the other children in the community.

In 1808 they moved to Kensington to be closer to the House chambers. William's departure from

Clapham was part of a process in which the community was becoming less lively and beneficial than it had been. For sixteen years, though, Clapham had contributed immensely to his spiritual well-being and persistence in his various endeavors.

After the Wilberforce family had settled in their new home, William hoped that national and world events might once again allow him to make some serious headway with his lifework, the abolition of slavery.

> The end of a matter is better than its beginning,
> and patience is better than pride.
>
> ECCLESIASTES 7:8 NIV

16

A NEW CENTURY

In terms of the hope for abolishing the slave trade, the nineteenth century began as the previous one had ended. The opposition was still stronger than those who supported Wilberforce, but he had no intention of giving up. Admittedly, the abolition movement was weak; Thomas Clarkson was no longer actively involved, and the Committee for the Abolition of the Slave Trade was dormant. William Pitt had been supportive in the early years of the effort, but it appeared that he could no longer be counted on for support. But other events seemed more hopeful. The war with France was looking less threatening. The price of sugar had dropped by about half, opening the plantation owners to discussions about ending the slave trade as a means of preventing other nations from gaining an advantage.

While some planters indicated a willingness to discuss the voluntary suspension of the trade for five years, in the final analysis they feared they would never be able to revive the trade after that passage of time. Negotiations with the planters preoccupied Wilberforce during 1800, and he did not introduce an abolition bill in that session. Likewise, in 1801, Wilberforce did not introduce a new bill, instead concentrating on the possibility that peace negotiations with France might open the way for the coordinated ending of the slave trade by both nations. Developments in 1802 and 1803 were no more encouraging. A bill to restrict slave importation to already-developed lands was defeated in Commons, and England was preoccupied with the renewal of the war with France in 1803.

Wilberforce and Pitt often discussed political tactics concerning the slave trade. Pitt, always the pragmatist, thought it unwise to ask the House of Lords to take up the bill.

"Let's assume for the moment that it's not practical or possible to take the abolition bill to the Lords," Wilberforce said to Pitt. "Are there other steps that can be taken?"

"I think the king might be persuaded to enter an Order in Council to stop the slave trade to Dutch Guiana, which we took from Holland during the war. Our planters couldn't object to curtailing the development of this colony. The Dutch will want the colony back after the war, and we could make it a condition of its return that Holland entirely stop its participation in the slave trade."

"I see your point about taking even a small step and doing it by royal proclamation, rather than having it drag on in the Parliament again. This is a matter of international diplomacy and needs an executive action. If you will proceed toward that end, Pitt, I will be grateful."

Pitt and Wilberforce had been able to work together on many political causes, though there were points at which Wilberforce's acts of conscience had been a disappointment to Pitt. In this case Wilberforce had reason to be disappointed in Pitt, for Pitt delayed for months the initiative they had discussed with regard to Dutch Guiana. During this time Pitt became more and more depressed with developments in the war with Napoleon, and illness took its toll on him. In spite of their political differences,

Wilberforce remained Pitt's devoted friend and never lost hope that there might be a chance to persuade him that he needed to surrender his soul and his life to Christ. Unfortunately, Bishop Pretyman served as Pitt's spiritual gatekeeper during his final illness, not allowing Wilberforce to come and pray with Pitt for his salvation. Wilberforce was given a prominent place in the funeral procession into Westminster Abbey, but the loss of his friend Pitt and the end of any chance to minister to him spiritually made this a very sad day for Wilberforce.

Ironically, Pitt's death became the first step toward the triumph of the abolition cause. Pitt's successor as prime minister was his cousin Lord Grenville, who had joined Pitt in encouraging Wilberforce to take up the slave trade cause in 1787. Grenville remained an ardent supporter of abolition when he assumed office. The Cabinet of the Grenville government included two other strong abolitionists: Charles James Fox, Foreign Secretary, and Lord Henry Petty, Chancellor of the Exchequer. These and other abolitionist voices in the new government outnumbered their opponents on the slave trade question.

WILLIAM WILBERFORCE ON "GOOD PEOPLE"

In reality, however, these people were never much concerned with spiritual matters, and while their external lives appear settled and happy, they still have no interest in a life of faith. They have no interest in the great work of their salvation, for they are preoccupied with earning money and raising their families. Meanwhile, they congratulate themselves on becoming so righteous, for they no longer commit the sins of their youth. In reality, however, they're not even tempted to commit these sins anymore, so how can their abstinence be considered any test of their moral characters?

James Stephen came to Wilberforce with a new idea. "William, this may sound like heresy, but I've been working with some trusted advisors and we would like you to hold off for a bit on filing your bill. You're aware that Pitt finally moved ahead on the Order in Council to stop the further importing of slaves to Dutch Guiana. That proclamation needs to be confirmed in Parliament, and this will be seen as very routine. The planters have already given it their support, since they don't want future competition from the Dutch in the Caribbean. So it will be a government bill, and it will move right through the Commons and the Lords. Here's the part that matters. We will ask Grenville to attach your Foreign Slave Bill to the measure, outlawing the carrying of slaves in British ships to any foreign destinations. We will make sure the abolitionists vote for the measure, and we know the government's supporters who are not opposed to slavery will also back the measure."

The first step in the new tactic for getting the abolition bill passed worked as planned. The Dutch Guiana measure passed handily in both houses, seeming to the proslavery interests to be of no significant harm. Behind the scenes, the abolitionists were planning for the second stage. It was May, and Parliament would be adjourning soon, but Wilberforce and Stephen wanted to press on. They concluded that Wilberforce should not be the one to bring the measure to the Commons. Fox would do it there, and Grenville would take it to the Lords. Wilberforce acknowledged that he probably had made too many enemies in his years of political battles and that the two key figures in the new government would be in a stronger position to introduce the measure. He persuaded Grenville and Fox to do their part in this process while he concentrated on composing a plea to the king, calling on him to use the coming peace negotiations as an opportunity to persuade the other European powers to follow England's lead in ending the trade.

In the debate in the Commons, Fox spoke of abolition as an accomplishment that would be well worth his forty years' work in the Parliament. The measure passed easily, and Wilberforce's appeal to the king succeeded as well. As he lay dying that summer, Fox again looked to the hope that the remaining steps toward abolition would be taken soon and expressed pleasure that he had been able to help the cause. In two years Wilberforce had lost two of the colleagues with whom he had agreed much of the time and with whom he had disagreed a good bit, too. In both cases, he was sad that they had not found the personal faith in Christ that was so central to his own life.

Even though Grenville had done his part by assuring that the abolition measure passed in the Lords, the session ended without its becoming law. The abolitionists expected this to happen but felt it was important to enter the new session in as strong a position as possible. Between sessions, Grenville called a general election.

Wilberforce returned to Yorkshire and campaigned energetically, convincing potential opponents that he had the support of the county. Grenville strengthened his support in the election as well.

Another project for Wilberforce during the recess was the writing of what started out to be a pamphlet and became a full-length book dealing with the slave trade and summarizing all of the arguments expressed by the abolitionists during the Parliament debates. It was his intention to have the book ready for the debate in the next session, and with the heroic efforts of the printer, he nearly accomplished it.

WILLIAM WILBERFORCE ON FAITH

Philosophy is designed only for those who are educated. It tends to divide society even more, breaking it into two parts: those who have money and leisure for learning, and those who don't. But—blessed be God—the faith that I am recommending was designed not for the rich but the poor. It removes the distinctions of class and wealth, and changes the condition of the entire social fabric. This faith makes all people useful members of civil society.

As had been agreed in developing the strategy the summer before, normal practice was to be reversed and Grenville would introduce the slave trade bill in the Lords first. He would try to head off a request for hearings, but by introducing the bill early in the session, there would be time for hearings if they were demanded. When the debate began in the Lords, two events helped build support. Wilberforce's book came out, and news came from the United States that Congress was moving ahead on an abolition bill. Moreover, the abolition committee had come back to life, urging members of Parliament to support the measure.

Grenville presented a strong speech in favor of the measure and ended with a personal tribute to Wilberforce, who was listening in the gallery:

> *I cannot conceive any consciousness more gratifying than must be enjoyed by that person [Wilberforce], on finding a measure to which he has devoted the labour of his life, carried into effect—a measure so truly benevolent, so admirably conducive to the virtuous prosperity of this country, and the welfare of mankind—a measure which will diffuse happiness amongst millions, now in existence, and for which his memory will be blessed by millions yet unborn.[46]*

The vote was surprisingly strong in the Lords, 100 for and 36 against. The remaining steps in the Lords' approval were taken without opposition, clearing the way for prompt action in the Commons. Wilberforce approached this step in the process feeling optimistic but taking nothing for granted. In the past he had brought the measures to the Commons himself, but this time the bill came from the Government with the impetus of its previous passage by the Lords. As the debate began, it soon became apparent that the bill would pass. Some opponents rose to speak, but the supporters were more numerous and more forceful. Wilberforce contributed briefly to the discussion, but he could see that the vote was at last going to go his way. Sir Samuel Romily echoed the praise the prime minister had given in the House of Lords, contrasting the great satisfaction that Wilberforce could take in his accomplishment with the feeling that Napoleon must have had in looking back on the suffering resulting from his conquests:

> When he [Wilberforce] compared with these pangs
> of remorse, the feeling which must accompany his
> hon. Friend from that house to his home, after
> the vote of that night should have confirmed the

*object of his humane and unceasing labours; when
he should retire into the bosom of his happy and
delighted family, when he should lay himself
down on his bed, reflecting on the innumerable
voices that would be raised in every quarter of
the world to bless him; how much more pure and
perfect felicity must he enjoy in the consciousness of
having preserved so many millions of his fellow-
creatures, than the man with whom he had compared him, on the throne to which he had waded
through slaughter and oppression.*[47]

So dramatically had the pendulum swung in the
direction of support for abolition that Romily's moving tribute brought forth an unprecedented standing
ovation from House members, with greater force
and enthusiasm than could be remembered for any
other member. After his twenty years of unrelenting
effort, Wilberforce fully deserved the tribute, but he
was completely overcome by it. All he could do was
sit weeping, thinking back to the time so many years
ago when he had decided that slavery was one of the
causes for which God had called him into public life.

It took another month for the process to be fully
completed, including committee action, third reading,

confirmation by the Lords, and royal assent. No one doubted the outcome during that stage, but Wilberforce breathed more freely when all of these steps had been completed.

"William," Thornton asked, "how do you feel now that you've finished what you set out to do?"

"Henry, I feel a lot of relief and gratitude to God, but we haven't finished much at all. If we could have ended slavery entirely and emancipated the slaves in the Empire, that would have been an accomplishment. I have every intention of going to work immediately to tackle the slavery problem. Righteousness will conquer evil. God will defeat the enemies. Someday we will have another celebration. If I'm in heaven then, there will be a huge chorus of angels at my side, rejoicing when the slaves are free."

> "See to it that you complete the work you have received in the Lord."
>
> COLOSSIANS 4:17 NIV

 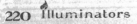

17

PASSING THE TORCH

Wilberforce had been thinking about the Sierra Leone colony, which he and Henry Thornton had actively supported over the years. Now that the slave trade had ended, he thought it would be appropriate for Sierra Leone to become an official British colony. That would facilitate the use of Freetown as a staging area for the navy in patrolling the coast to look for British ships whose owners might think they could get away with participating in the slave trade.

Wilberforce had already set things in motion for a public meeting to promote the founding of an "African Institute" whose goals would be the promotion of the civilization and improvement of all of Africa. He had talked with the Duke of Gloucester about hosting a meeting in the Freemasons' Hall to which they would invite many national leaders. Wilberforce believed the time was right to direct their energies to something immediately impacting the great continent of Africa.

Thornton agreed that the time was right to promote this more ambitious effort in Africa. They needed something more comprehensive than what they had been able to do in Sierra Leone. New and constructive openings for trade with Africa were needed, along with more opportunities for those Africans who chose to return to their homeland.

WILLIAM WILBERFORCE ON INTEGRITY

You cannot go forward a single step until you have become indifferent to what people will think of you. Make it your goal to seek always to please God. When the world's opinion is different from God's, remember that if you follow the world, you will never be truly respectable or good or happy.

Four years after the passage of the slave trade bill and the founding of the African Institution, Wilberforce paced back and forth in his room, pausing sometimes to drop to his knees in prayer, at other times to laboriously list the pros and cons of the decision he was facing. Thirty-one years ago he had been elected to Parliament, and now he faced a momentous choice. He saw three possibilities: continue his increasingly burdensome duties as they were, drop out of the Commons entirely, or resign from his seat representing Yorkshire to seek a small borough with fewer demands on his time.

Wilberforce talked with his Christian friends about the decision and found no clear agreement among them. Some could see that his health was declining and counseled him to leave politics entirely. He continued to struggle with colitis and had to maintain his regular doses of opium. He was also suffering from the early stages of curvature of the spine, and before long he would experience the annoying necessity of wearing a cumbersome leather brace with steel stays. One shoulder had begun to sag, and without determined effort, his head fell forward against his chest.

Also weighing on the side of leaving politics

were the challenges of being a good father to six children, the oldest of whom was then thirteen. He and Barbara had a number of governesses and tutors, but Wilberforce was not comfortable with the common practice among the wealthy of delegating the entire raising of children to their domestic staff. He loved reading to the children and playing games with them, even when they tended toward being out of control. During the busy times of Parliament's session, he found it hard to spend much time with them. Once when he picked up one of his sons, the boy began to cry. "He always is afraid of strangers," said the child's nurse, filling Wilberforce with guilt and sadness.[48]

Occasionally a constituent from Yorkshire would complain when Wilberforce did not respond to a letter on a timely basis. No matter how hard he tried, he could not keep up with his correspondence, nor could he find time to see everyone who came to him with their requests and complaints. He had fought for twenty years for the passage of the slave trade bill and had worked on numerous projects such as the Sierra Leone colony. Wilberforce was visibly exhausted.

As he prayed and made entries in his journal, his responsibility for his children's moral training weighed heavily on him. He wrote, "They claim a father's heart, eye, and voice, and friendly intercourse. Now so long as I am M.P. for Yorkshire, it will, I fear, be impossible for me to give my heart and time to the work as I ought, unless I become a negligent M.P. such as does not become our great country."[49] Adding to his concern for the children were Barbara's longstanding anxiety about his health and the stress his public life placed on the family.

Wilberforce took the middle ground in this hard decision, deciding to resign the Yorkshire seat and accept the offer of representing the small borough of Bramber in Sussex. Barbara's cousin Lord Calthorpe controlled the borough and was an admirer of Wilberforce. He was pleased to have William accept appointment from Bramber. This was not an easy thing for a person who had always supported the need for reform in an electoral system that made possible exactly the kind of "pocket borough" he was going to represent. Unlike William Pitt, who had entered Parliament from a pocket borough at the very beginning, Wilberforce had taken the high road in winning elections with legitimate campaigns.

But in the end Wilberforce decided to take the new position in the Commons, reasoning that he could still support parliamentary reform while availing himself of the opportunity to continue his career without the enormous demands of a huge constituency.

The family's move to a house in Kensington, a mile from the parliamentary buildings, decreased his travel time but increased the problem of constituents showing up at his house asking for help of various sorts. Wilberforce loved to be with people and tolerated the chaos that resulted from his many visitors. But Barbara was relieved when he resigned from the Yorkshire seat, hoping there would be fewer intrusions into their home life.

WILLIAM WILBERFORCE ON DISCIPLINE

Don't let your precious time be wasted by shapeless laziness. These days, even the most spiritual of us tend to have a relaxed attitude about spiritual discipline. Instead, use your time and energy wisely, as good stewards. Never be satisfied with your present achievement, but "forgetting the things which are behind," work to "press forward" with undiminished energy, running the race that is set before you without ever flagging.

William and Barbara's devotion to their children was amply rewarded by the success of three of their four sons, who each went to the strongest college at Oxford, earned honors, and took up careers as clergymen. As university students they applied themselves in ways that William wished he had done at Cambridge. But the pathway of their oldest son, William, was quite a different matter. In his early years in school, he was not a good student and sometimes acted in immature ways. At Cambridge young William was even less diligent in his studies than his father had been. He spent money wastefully, lied to his parents, and disgraced them by getting drunk after his friend died and was awaiting burial. The elder William blamed himself for his son's waywardness, writing in his journal as follows:

> *O my poor William. How strange he can make so miserable those who love him best and whom really he loves. His soft nature makes him the sport of his companions, and the wicked and idle naturally attach themselves like dust and cleave like burrs. I go to pray for him. Alas, could I love my Savior more and serve him, God would hear my prayer and turn his heart.*[50]

Wilberforce's agonized prayers for his eldest son were answered in the sense that their relationship remained strong and young William did not become completely prodigal. The elder William felt he must remove his son from Cambridge until he became more serious about his studies, but he never returned to the university. He undertook legal studies with a friend of his father but did not do well in studying the law, either.

In the nine years Wilberforce represented the Bramber borough, he was able to slow his pace somewhat because of the reduced demands from constituents, but he continued with a variety of causes on the floor of the Commons. He worked unsuccessfully to eliminate the ban on Catholics serving in the House of Commons. He was successful in his campaign to allow Christian missionaries to be admitted to service in India. He was unsuccessful in bringing about England's recognition of Haiti but provided encouragement and assistance to King Christophe of the new republic of Haiti.

While he worked on these and other causes in Parliament, Wilberforce's passion continued to be the emancipation of the slaves in England's colonies and, if possible, in all European colonies. He tried two strategies, neither of which was successful, but both of which helped keep the issue alive. One was the effort to require that a register of slaves be kept by colonial administrators. This was meant to assist in documenting the illegal importation of slaves. The slave interests in the colonies opposed this effort in Parliament. Later the colonial legislatures passed measures requiring that registers of slaves be kept, but the legislators passed these bills with no intention of implementing them.

Wilberforce and his allies in the emancipation effort also worked on the diplomatic front, lobbying participants in the European peacemaking conferences to include a provision in the treaty ending the Napoleonic wars that would ban any European participation in the slave trade. Nothing was accomplished at first, but then Napoleon took power again in France and abolished the slave trade in the French Empire in an effort to win support from England. When Louis XVIII was restored to the throne of France, he confirmed Napoleon's abolition decree and an abolition provision was added to the treaties coming from the Congress of Vienna. Things are not always as they seem, however, for none of the eight participants in the peace discussions, except England, made any effort to stop the slave trade.

The failure of these efforts strengthened the determination of the antislavery forces in England to press for the goal they would have desired from the beginning, the complete emancipation of slaves in the British Empire. But Wilberforce was experiencing more frequent health problems, and it became apparent to him that he must find someone younger to carry on the work in Parliament. Many of those who had been a part of the abolition core group from Clapham were no longer alive, and the loss of Henry Thornton, who had died in 1815, was especially painful.

Wilberforce's search for an heir apparent was rewarded when he met Thomas Buxton, who won election to the Commons in 1818. The two men had much in common as both were from merchant families and both were committed evangelicals. Buxton took up causes that connected well with Wilberforce's values, including prison reform, the improvement of working conditions in industry, and the abolition of the death penalty. Buxton had numerous connections with the Quakers, who had been consistent backers of abolition and emancipation. Buxton's sister-in-law, Elizabeth Fry, was a strong leader in prison reform and a zealous Quaker reformer in other ways.

Wilberforce discussed the situation with Buxton. "I may have to retire from Parliament before long, and I would like to start working with someone from within the Commons who would take up the cause. There are still plenty of people working behind the scenes, but someone will be needed in Parliament to take the lead, just as I attempted to do with the abolition effort more than thirty years ago. Thomas, I'm asking you to consider being that person."

"I'm sure you realize I'm not nearly as well versed on the slavery issue as I am regarding some other causes. I honestly don't know if I'm the one to take up your mantle, but I'm deeply touched that you've asked me. I can't give you an immediate answer, but I will pray carefully about it. Please pray with me that I will be led to the right decision."

Wilberforce was not idle while Buxton made his decision. In early 1823 Wilberforce helped organize a large rally to generate support for the new Anti-Slavery Society, the goal of which was to generate popular support for the complete emancipation of the slaves. Wilberforce wrote a pamphlet in support of emancipation and presented a petition calling on Parliament to abolish slavery.

WORLD EVENTS OF 1823

Simón Bolívar is named president of Peru.

New York City politician William "Boss" Tweed is born in Manhattan.

English physician Edward Jenner, a pioneer in the smallpox vaccine, dies.

U.S. president James Monroe proclaims his "Monroe Doctrine," warning European powers against interfering with the affairs of the Americas.

After some months of thought and prayer, Buxton agreed to take up Wilberforce's work on emancipation. That opened the way for Wilberforce to begin making a graceful exit from the national political stage. In remarks to the Anti-Slavery Society in mid-1824, he gave a sort of benediction to his work:

We have been engaged in many a long and arduous contest, and we also have had to contend with calumny and falsehood. But we are more than

repaid, by the success that has already attended our
efforts, and by the anticipations which we may
derive from what we have witnessed this very
day, when, if our sun be setting, we see that other
luminaries are arising to shine with far greater
lustre and more efficient strength.[51]

> The LORD works righteousness and
> justice for all the oppressed.
>
> PSALM 103:6 NIV

18

ABIDING ELOQUENCE

As Wilberforce's health deteriorated, he realized he must resign from Parliament. Although Thomas Buxton reminded Wilberforce that the antislavery forces still needed his courageous spirit, not to mention the great respect he had in Commons and among the people, he was firm in the decision.

"There will be times when we need you to stand up and use your incomparable powers of persuasion," Buxton assured him.

If legislation were not to move forward without him, Wilberforce would have been deeply disappointed, for his body could no longer keep up with his spirit. But within a short amount of time, Buxton showed himself to be a good choice to carry the cause of emancipation in the Commons. "I may not live to see the final conquest, but God's righteousness will be restored in our land, at least in this respect. I have no doubt of that."

WILLIAM WILBERFORCE ON PASSION

In the true Christian, everything is full of life and motion, and the great work to do excites the various passions of the soul. No one should imagine that the Christian life is a state of boring toil and hardship. The Christian's work is "the labours of love," and if "he has need of patience," it is "the patience of hope." He is cheered in his work by the constant assurance of God's present support and ultimate victory. Faith fills our life on earth with meaning, even as it gives us hope for eternity.

Had Wilberforce felt free to follow his wife's preferences, he would have stepped down long ago. She felt it her duty to protect him from further physical suffering and an untimely death. Now he could see that his ailments were causing her anxiety, and though he could continue to endure some suffering himself, he did not want to bring more on her.

"Our worth as Christians is not in our power and prestige, Buxton, but in our relationship with the heavenly Father. When we feel led to pass our work on to others, we can be sure that the same God who called us to this work will raise up others to carry it on. I'm delighted that you have accepted part of the work, and there are many others who will help. As a follower of Christ, I can trust that the work of the kingdom of God will get done in God's time. My time in this work has come and gone, and I must say I have great peace about laying aside the office I hold and giving myself more diligently to my family and other causes."

Wilberforce had earned the quieter life to which he now turned. He established a routine of saying daily prayers, hearing his correspondence read, conversing with family and friends, and answering his letters. He was able to enjoy the accomplishments of his children, although he had to continue struggling with the misfortunes of his oldest son. Young William studied for the bar but abandoned his studies when ill health hindered his diligence. With major financial backing from his father and loans from numerous others, young William bought a dairy farm and a retail milk business. It had the potential to support his family, but in a short time the business failed and his debts multiplied.

Young William then headed for Europe to get away from his creditors. His father could have left it to others to deal with his son, but he felt compelled to take responsibility for the debts. He sold the farm he had bought when they left London, as well as the family lands in Yorkshire, leaving him with no home and little income. He made a virtue out of a necessity, however, professing to enjoy the simplification of his life and the chance to spend time with each of his children.

In the late 1820s and early 1830s, Buxton and the emancipation group in Parliament continued their efforts with little success. Nevertheless, popular support continued to grow, as evidenced by the turnout of two thousand people at the 1830 Anti-Slavery meeting. Wilberforce participated in the rally, though he was physically weak. Three years later he made his last public appearance, speaking out once again in support of emancipation. He was extremely frail, but he reached deep inside for some of the passion that had always characterized his work on behalf of the slaves.

July 26, 1833

"Some folks spend their whole lives working toward some important end and are not blessed to see its accomplishment," William thought to himself as he

WORLD EVENTS OF 1833

The town of Chicago, population 350, is incorporated.

Isabella II, infant daughter of Maria Cristina, is named queen of Spain.

Composer Johannes Brahms is born in Germany.

Benjamin Harrison, twenty-third president of the United States, is born in Ohio.

Alfred Nobel, inventor of dynamite and founder of the Nobel Prize, is born in Sweden.

watched through the window as Zachary Macaulay's carriage drove away. Yesterday the House had passed on second reading the measure to abolish slavery. The Lords would certainly concur, and he knew the king would agree to the measure as well. Moreover, the government had agreed to dip into the treasury to assure that the slave owners had the money to seek more honorable economic pursuits.

He folded his hands together and closed his eyes. "Should it be the desire of my heavenly Father to take me home shortly, I shall go with great rejoicing." A few hours later, William Wilberforce died.

Shortly after his death, Barbara Wilberforce expressed a perspective on her husband's death reflective of his great trust in God and and her high regard for him:

> Why should I wish to detain in a sinking, emaciated suffering body, such a spirit from eternal joys, from a state where pain and sorrow and above all sin, are to be known no more? My loss is indeed beyond measure and expression great, but to him, I trust, it is unspeakable gain and I ought to be full of thankfulness that such a treasure was spared to me, to his family, to his country and to the world

so long, and recalled at last with so little compara-
tive suffering, especially of acute pain, which the
exquisite sensibility of his delicate frame so little
enabled him to cope with.[52]

WILLIAM WILBERFORCE ON SOCIAL DUTY

I call on all of you who are true Christians, then, to
work together earnestly to prove the worth of your
profession, putting to silence the empty ridicule of
ignorant objectors. Boldly stand up for the cause of
Christ in an age when so many who bear the name
of Christ are ashamed of Him. On your shoulders
rests your country's fate; it is up to you to suspend
its fall. In the end, however, we can never be certain
of the political outcome of our actions—but nevertheless, without a doubt, restoring the influence of
faith and raising the moral standard will have sure
and radical benefits for us all.

On the statue of William Wilberforce in Westminster Abbey, where he was buried, are these words:

In an age and country fertile in great and good men, he was among the foremost of those who fixed the character of their times because to high and various talents, to warm benevolence, and to universal candour, he added the abiding eloquence of a Christian life.[53]

The word suggested by this epitaph and by William Wilberforce's entire life is *extraordinary*. In no way does it exaggerate the significance of his life to use this word to characterize who he was and what he accomplished:

EXTRAORDINARY SPIRITUAL REBIRTH—Wilberforce had been an undisciplined, spoiled rich child who did only enough during his years in school and at Cambridge University to get by and graduate. He reached his goals of having a good time and making friends. Within a few years, he made his way out of the emptiness of his life into a transforming experience with Jesus Christ as Savior and Lord. He never stopped being witty and personable, but his life took on a seriousness and dedication he had never experienced before. He was a different man, and his spiritual life became the single most important part of who he was from that time forward.

EXTRAORDINARY FOCUS—Wilberforce entered politics for lack of anything better to do. He had no goals, no passion, and no issues. After he committed his life to Christ, he sought a purpose in politics and found it in the ambitious goals of transforming British moral conduct and bringing an end to the single greatest human evil of the day, slavery. He became involved with many issues and projects in his career, but from beginning to end he remained focused on moral reform and emancipation.

EXTRAORDINARY ELECTORAL SUCCESS—When Wilberforce made the giant leap from representing Hull to winning one of the most prestigious seats in the Commons, representing Yorkshire, he did so with very little apparent forethought or plan. But he had charisma, great oratorical skill, and superb timing. His success in winning the seat and holding it throughout his battle against slavery was extremely important in providing him political longevity and power.

EXTRAORDINARY IMPACT ON HUMAN BEHAVIOR—
Wilberforce never intended to limit his efforts to the
slavery problem. His early conviction was that God
had also called him to work in the private sector,
through such channels as the Proclamation Societies,
to turn people toward more upright living. He and his
fellow believers in Parliament and other leadership
positions continued to set a strong example of integrity and godly living, impacting the national character
in ways that are hard to measure but still significant.

EXTRAORDINARY DETERMINATION TO ELIMINATE
SLAVERY—Twenty years is a long time to work on
one issue, especially when it was apparent to most
abolitionists that their real goal was emancipation.
The defeats in Parliament before the ultimate
victory were almost too many to count. For Wilberforce to achieve the abolition victory and then
begin immediately to work on emancipation is most
amazing. He had no way of knowing the second goal
would take another twenty-six years, but in a way it
didn't matter to Wilberforce. He was convinced it
was essential to reach the goal and had no thought
of giving up.

EXTRAORDINARY IMPACT THROUGH HIS BOOK—
Politicians and other activists don't often have time to
write books, much less to write good and successful
books. Wilberforce's book on Christian living made a
major impact on his contemporaries and still is a useful guide to Christian conduct. He applied the same
determination in getting the book done that he did
in pursuing political goals. He had very little time to
write, but he got it done, and an entire generation was
influenced by it.

EXTRAORDINARY SURVIVAL PHYSICALLY—
Wilberforce's illnesses as a young man made it appear that he would not live long, especially since the
doctors had only a vague notion of the source of his
pain. The doctors prescribed opium, and with God's
help and his own self-discipline, he was able to avoid
becoming addicted to the drug and continued its daily
use to control the pain from his digestive ailments. He
outlived many of his contemporaries in spite of the
stressful life he lived. He was a walking example of
God's grace and healing.

EXTRAORDINARY DIVERSITY OF INTERESTS—
Wilberforce is primarily remembered for his work against slavery, but his involvement in other causes was almost limitless, inside and outside the government. He sought to help the victims of society—the orphans, single mothers, and chimney sweeps. He was active in a long list of Christian groups, including the Society for Bettering the Cause of the Poor, the Church Missionary Society, the British and Foreign Bible Society, the African Institute, and the Anti-Slavery Society. Someone attempted to count the charitable groups he assisted with his efforts and his philanthropy and came up with a list of sixty-nine groups.

EXTRAORDINARY DEATH—To be lucid and personable two days before he died was an amazing gift for a person who endured many physical problems. God honored Wilberforce's faithfulness and determination by allowing him to live until Parliament had voted on the emancipation bill and it was certain to pass. His work of fifty years was accomplished, and he could go to meet Jesus with a keen sense of "the abiding eloquence of a Christian life."

And now these three remain: faith, hope and love. But the greatest of these is love.

1 CORINTHIANS 13:13 NIV

NOTES

1. Robin Furneaux, *William Wilberforce* (London: Hamish Hamilton, 1974), 8.
2. John Pollock, *William Wilberforce* (London: Constable, 1977), 6.
3. Garth Lean, *God's Politician: William Wilberforce's Struggle* (London: Darton, Longman & Todd, 1980), 12.
4. Furneaux, 11.
5. Pollock, 27.
6. Furneaux, 30.
7. Ibid., 36.
8. Ibid., 37–38.
9. Lean, 37.
10. Pollock, 41.
11. Ibid.
12. Lean, 42.
13. Ibid., 44.
14. Pollock, 50.
15. Ibid., 51.
16. Furneaux, 70.

17. Ibid., 70.

18. Ibid.

19. Furneaux, 73–75.

20. Lean, 51.

21. Pollock, 47.

22. Lean, 73–77.

23. Pollock, 61.

24. Lean, 88–91

25. Furneaux, 99.

26. Pollock, 119–20.

27. Ibid., 118.

28. Lean, 106.

29. William Wilberforce, *Real Christianity: Contrasted with the Prevailing Religious System* (Portland, OR: Multnomah Press, 1982), xvi.

30. Pollock, 122.

31. Ibid., 130–31.

32. Furneaux, 184.

33. Pollock, 47

34. Ibid., 82.

35. Furneaux, 95.

36. Ibid., 109.

37. Ibid., 111.

38. Wilberforce, 1.

39. Ibid., 30.

40. Ibid., 41.
41. Ibid., 130–31.
42. Furneaux, 151–52.
43. Pollock, 149.
44. Lean, 134.
45. Furneaux, 162.
46. Ibid., 250.
47. Ibid., 253.
48. Ibid., 314.
49. Ibid., 315.
50. Pollock, 267.
51. Ibid., 290.
52. Furneaux, 455.
53. Ibid., 456.

INDEX OF EXCERPTS

ABOUT THE AUTHOR

Lon Fendall directs the Center for Global Studies at George Fox University in Newberg, Oregon. He has served as a youth director, a college professor, and a dean, as well as on the staffs of a U.S. Senator and World Vision. Lon and his wife, Raelene, have been married more than forty years.

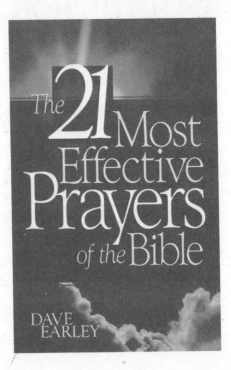